D1404479

Crafts From Other Cultures

written and illustrated by Judy Hierstein

FS-10146 Crafts From Other Cultures
All rights reserved–Printed in the U.S.A.
Copyright © 1994 Frank Schaffer Publications, Inc.
23740 Hawthorne Blvd.
Torrance, CA 90505

Table of Contents

China

Terra Cotta Warriors 2
Chinese Papercuts and Taoism 6
Chinese Opera and Masks 8
Chinese Calligraphy and Painting 10
Shadow Puppets 14
Chinese New Year and the Dragons 16
Chinese Symbols and the Zodiac 18
The Art of Chinese Cooking 20
Bibliography 22

India

The Indus Valley Civilization 24
Hinduism 26
Hindu Music and Dance 28
Elephants 30
Muslims and the Taj Mahal 32
Indian Weddings 34
Appliqued Felt Rugs From Kashmir 36
Cotton and Silk Production, Clothing 38
Indian Cooking 40
Bibliography 42

Mexico

Ancient Indian Civilization 44
Mayan Weaving on Backstrap Looms 46
Spanish Invasion 48
The Marketplace 50
Terra Cotta Tiles and Lanterns 52
Flowers 54
The Sacred Paper of San Pablito 56
Modern-Day Murals 58
Mexican Cooking 60
Bibliography 62

Russia

Icons 64
Mosaics 66
Windows and Woodcarving 68
Babushkas and Bread Dough 70
St. Basil's Cathedral 72
The Bolshoi Ballet 74
Eggs, Eggs, and Eggs 76
Chess 78
Russian Cooking 80
Bibliography 82

Australia

Aboriginal Rock Painting 84
Totems and Bark Painting 86
An Ancient Aboriginal LifeStyle 88
Boomerangs, Corroborees, and Didjeridus 90
Through English Eyes 92
Authentic Australian 94
Great Barrier Reef 96
Sydney Opera House 98
Dinner Down Under 100
Bibliography 102

Africa

The Fabric of Africa 104
Funeral Fabric 106
Cokwe Basketry 108
Golden Ornaments 110
Masks, Masks, and More Masks 112
Home Sweet Village 116
Now This Story 118
West African Eating 120
Bibliography 122

The Last Word.. 123

*For Clay Recipes, see page 4.

To The Teacher

The purpose of this book is to provide the intermediate classroom teacher with ideas to enrich his or her class' study of other lands by using the native crafts of those lands.

The arts and crafts produced by any culture tell much about the way the people of that culture view the world. Many art and craft objects have (or had) religious significance, or tell ancient stories that have been passed down through generations. Lifestyles of a people are also evident in their artforms–a nomadic people may add rich and lavish decorations to adorn the everyday objects they must carry from place to place, while less nomadic cultures may produce less mobile art. More affluent cultures have more time to devote to artistic endeavors than those whose main concern is staying alive. Native crafts reflect the materials available in that particular area, but also show the influence of visiting strangers. Indeed, history itself can be taught by looking carefully at a culture's art.

This book focuses on six countries: Africa, China, India, Mexico, Australia, and Russia their art forms, and how they reflect the ideas and beliefs of their people. Some traditional art forms are translated into projects that teachers can do with students, or students can work on individually.

Since cooking is also a "craft" and tells much about a culture, some customs associated with food and several simple recipes are included. (Mastering chopsticks is quite an art in itself!) Holidays all over the world are traditionally celebrated with artfully decorated delicacies which hold special meaning for the people who celebrate them.

The world is growing ever smaller due to technological advances in communication, and all cultures are becoming increasingly alike. It seems all kids everywhere wear blue jeans, tennis shoes, and eat hamburgers. It is, therefore, more important than ever before that we teach our children about the rich cultural differences in people all over the earth.

China

Throughout China's long history, its people have never considered art to be separate from life. From the very rich to the very poor, the Chinese have always made and used objects with an aesthetic sense of "righteousness." Whether these objects were utilitarian for everyday living, or ceremonial for festivals or funerals and burial of the dead, whether simple or ornate, they were formed with great care to produce a pleasing appearance. Art was meant for all, to lead people's thoughts away from life's drudgeries to all that is beautiful in life and nature.

Terra Cotta Warriors

Much is known about China's past from excavations of tombs. Some of the oldest objects found are bronze ornamental vessels used to hold food and wine for the dead. These were often shaped like animals and decorated with symbols thought to protect the spirit. These objects are very beautiful and tell us that the Chinese placed great importance on the after-life.

As in ancient India, servants of wealthy Chinese 2,000 years ago were buried along with their masters. Luckily for the servants, this practice was changed and live servants were replaced with small clay replicas. Some of the figures were musicians playing instruments to entertain the dead, and even miniature dwellings were buried in the tombs. These figures give us clues about how people lived and what their homes looked like.

Then in 211 B.C., Qin Shi Huang became the Emperor of the Qin Dynasty by conquering the six warring states and established China as one unified nation. He was ruthless and unpopular, enforcing strict legal codes, imposing taxes, and silencing intellectual critics, but he completed the Great Wall to protect China from outside forces. It was his dynasty, the Qin Dynasty (pronounced "shin") which gave China its name.

Qin Shi Huang's most spectacular achievement, his terra cotta army, was discovered in 1974 by three farmers near Xi`an who were digging a well. Qin Shi Huang wanted to be more than just the first Emperor of the beginning of history; he wanted to be the greatest ruler in the Netherworld. So the year he became emperor, he began building his tomb bigger than any tomb before. Instead of including small figures of servants, as was common, he had an entire army of warriors formed from clay.

Each of these over 7,000 terra cotta warriors is different from the others. There are generals, officers, warriors, and cavalrymen of various ranks. Each figure is a unique work of art with realistic facial expressions showing joy, anger, grief, or solemn respect, and each body differs in size, shape, and height. It is as if actual warriors in Qins's army were used as models. The craftsmen made legs and feet solid and the upper bodies and heads hollow to make the figures stable. The tomb itself is modeled after the ancient city of Xi`an. It was once the eastern end of the Silk Road traveled by Marco Polo and still exists nearby. There are also horses and chariots buried there as well as many weapons that were used in those days.

Activities and Projects

Warriors

Using any moldable substance such as cooked dough, salt clay (see recipes below), oil modeling clay, or actual terra cotta itself, have students create their own warriors. This may be an individual project in which the student selects the size of the finished piece, a small group project, or an entire class project in which students recreate the tomb as it now appears unearthed near Xi'an. (Excavations are still underway, with new discoveries being made all the time.)

Use the pinching method to form the bottom half of the figure. Make it solid for stability as the artisans of the Qin Dynasty did. Roll a slab into a tube-shape to form the body. Add the arms, hands, and head. Use clay tools, toothpicks, plastic forks, Popsicle sticks, and sharpened dowels to add details. Fire the terra cotta figures if a kiln is available, though this is not necessary unless the figures are meant to last another 2,000 years!

Because traces of paint were detected on some of the figures, we know that they were originally painted, but after over 2,000 years, they appear a warm clay beige color with darker shades in the grooves and crevices. Students can determine which finish they prefer. Paint the figures realistically or clay-beige all over with tempera or acrylics. Then add a darker brown to the cracks and crevices, wiping off the excess. In China small slip-cast replicas are covered with mud and then lightly buffed to make them appear aged! This is a good method to achieve an authentic look.

Cooked Dough—Combine 1 cup flour, 1/2 cup salt, 1 cup water, 2 teaspoons cream of tartar, and 1 tablespoon oil in a saucepan and cook over moderate heat, stirring constantly until mixture thickens. May be molded as soon as it is cool enough. Keep wrapped in plastic until used.

Salt Clay—Mix 4 cups flour and 1 cup salt thoroughly, then add 1-1/4 cups water and mix. Mixture will be stiff enough to knead.

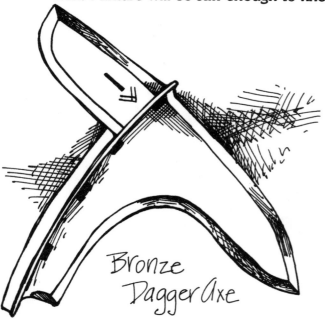

Bronze Dagger Axe

Weapons

The warriors were all equipped with bronze weapons of one kind or another. These included crossbows, spears, dagger axes, halberds, battle axes, swords, curved knives, and two ancient Chinese weapons, *shu* and *pi*. Have a student or small group research these and the history of weaponry in China and illustrate findings on large posters. How does the evolution of weapons in China compare to that of Western civilization? Was there any exchange of technology? For example, the Chinese invented gunpowder, but the Europeans were the ones who thought to use it as a weapon.

5

Chinese Papercuts and Taoism

Taoism, or Daoism, is an ancient Chinese philosophy attributed to Lao Tzu. The word *Tao* means "the way," and Taoists believe that the way to happiness is back to nature. They believe we should rid ourselves of artificial restraints and useless possessions and live in simplicity and goodness like children.

Chuang Tzu was a famous Taoist philosopher who lived in the fourth and third centuries B.C. He wrote of a dream he had in which he was a butterfly floating softly from flower to flower sipping nectar. Then he woke up. He was Chuang Tzu again. Or was he? Perhaps he was still a butterfly dreaming he was Chuang Tzu.

He also wrote of a young man who was chasing a butterfly and accidentally ran into a garden, where he saw a beautiful young woman and immediately fell in love with her. He vowed to work hard and win her father's approval and her love. Eventually they were married and, of course, lived happily ever after.

The butterfly is a popular symbol in China. It is a symbol of joy and summertime as in the first story, and it is also a Chinese cupid figure, as in the second. For these reasons and for its beauty, it is often seen on Chinese porcelain, embroidery, and in papercuts.

Papercutting is a delicate and beautiful handcraft in China. Artists work with small scissors and cut unbelievably intricate pictures out of thin red or black paper. They may be any size, shape, or subject matter. These are then mounted on paper of a contrasting color, usually white. Sometimes they are cut from tissue paper, then touched lightly with a thin watercolor wash which bleeds to the edges.

Activities and Projects

Study the examples of Chinese papercut butterflies shown on the following page. Using a lightweight paper, cut a butterfly of your own. You may want to try cutting with a pair of scissors or an Exacto knife. A paper punch may be helpful for some difficult inside details. When the cutting is completed, dampen the entire surface, add watercolor sparingly, and watch it bleed.

Design a larger papercut project. Make sketches on a circle 6"–12" in diameter. Look at books about Chinese art for ideas and motifs. You may want to combine Chinese decorative borders, calligraphy, and animals. You must plan your papercut with enough edges touching one another so the art will not fall apart when finished. Mount your finished work by spraying the back lightly with spray adhesive and carefully placing the background face down on top of it. Once the piece is down it cannot be easily repositioned.

Chinese Opera and Masks

Traditional Chinese opera began in the fourteenth century during the Yuan Dynasty. It was popular at weddings, births, funerals, and festivals for the entertainment of living guests and dead ancestors. The operas sometimes went on for weeks, and the audience would come and go as they wished, eating watermelon, sipping tea, singing, cheering, booing, and hissing.

Opera is comprised of music, singing, poetry and blank verse, pantomime, acrobatics, and dance all rolled into one. The plays are about great historical and mythical battles, filled with combat and violent deeds, or about more ordinary aspects of social life, highly moral and often comic. After the revolution, operas had to be acceptable to the national government, but today people enjoy traditional operas again.

Every aspect of Chinese opera is highly symbolic. The audience can tell the actor's character by the color of his makeup; red makeup means loyalty, white—treachery. Yellow indicates impulsiveness, while black denotes the character is honest, bold, and good, but a little uncouth. Silver and gold makeup is reserved for gods and demons.

The settings, props, and actors' gestures are all symbolic as well, and members of the audience know what each means, just as they know what the play is about before they get there. If a male character lifts his foot as he exits, that means he is stepping over a door's threshold, and if he puts his hands out in front of him, this indicates it is dark. It is common for a male actor to play a female role and vice versa. Perhaps the most well-known Chinese opera star, Mei Lafang, is famous for the female roles he has played. The costumes are so extensive and elaborate, and the makeup is so mask-like, that the gender of the actor makes little difference.

papier-mache

Activities and Projects ─────

Masks

Study the Chinese opera masks shown; then, using the same style, create masks. On a sheet of heavy paper that is about 2-1/2 times longer than it is wide (12" x 30" or 8" x 20") lightly sketch three egg shapes with the pointed side downward to represent a chin. Roughly sketch in the eyes, nose, and mouth and proceed to paint "makeup" onto the three masks with tempera or any other bright paint.

Repeat the project with papier-mache eggs. Blow up oval balloons and paste strips of newspaper or paper towels onto them with thin wallpaper paste. Paint them when they are completely dry. This makes an effective class project to display. Include ancient Chinese legends students obtain from research or invent one about each character mask.

Repeat the project in miniature with halves of plastic Easter eggs or wooden eggs.

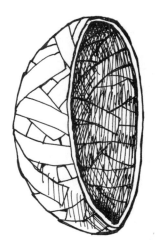

cut in half

Cut details from oaktag

Paint
Glue buttons, sequins, yarn, and scraps for decoration.

Mount on stiff cardboard or matboard.

Chinese Calligraphy and Painting

Chinese artists often paint landscapes but rarely from viewing them directly. Instead, they quietly contemplate nature until they feel they are at one with the spirit, or lifeforce, Chi, of every living thing, and then they try to capture this lifeforce on paper. They leave out what they feel is nonessential. Every stroke is carefully placed and is of utmost importance. Calligraphy in China is considered part of the same artform as painting. Both are done with a brush and special cake of ink which has been ground on a slate ink stone and mixed with water.

Paintings and calligraphy are done on paper scrolls, to be hung vertically or rolled horizontally. It is not uncommon to see a combination of illustration and calligraphy on one scroll. The artist may paint a scene, then add a poem or comment. When the work is finished, he/she adds a "chop" (a signature stamp) in a special bright red ink. If the work is given as a gift, the recipient may add his/her own comments or thoughts about the work and his/her own chop. This does not destroy the work but adds to its value.

water well

ink grinding surface

Slate ink stone

Cake of ink

bamboo brush

Chinese writing, like Egyptian hieroglyphics, originated in the form of pictograms. It is said to have been invented around 3000 B.C. by Ts`and Chieh when he observed the footprints of birds in the sand. The pictures gradually changed to ideograms which have meaning alone or in combination with others. There are over 40,000 separate characters, but many have become obsolete. Most books can be read with an understanding of about 4,000. There are many different languages and dialects spoken in China, but the written language is the same, since each character represents an idea rather than a sound. The people in China can understand one another so long as they all write it down! Some characters are now being replaced with characters that represent sounds.

On Chinese New Year, the people hang on their doors decorated red banners with good luck wishes written vertically in Chinese characters. Many are such old and traditional phrases that it is difficult to translate them literally, but everyone understands what they mean.

Evolution of Chinese Pictograms

Early Form	⌃⌃	👁	🧍	🌲🌲	🐂	🐑
English Word	Hills	Eye	Child	Forest	Ox	Sheep
Modern Form	屵屵	目	子	林	牛	羊

Early Form	🐍	🐟	🐦	🐸	🐘	🐴
English Word	Snake	Fish	Bird	Toad	Elephant	Horse
Modern Form	蛇	魚	鳥	蛙	象	馬

Chinese Calligraphy on New Year's Good Luck Banners

Big Luck on Your Head

Year after Year - Big Luck

Money Coming Without Difficulties

Activities and Projects

Create Your Own Chop

Chinese chops come in all sizes. They may be quite small (1/2" x 1/2") and purely utilitarian, simply for adding a signature, or they may be rather large and ornately carved from stone in the shape of animals or elaborate designs. Some chops are works of art in themselves.

Invent some "Chinese" characters to represent how your own name might look or ask someone who knows Chinese to write your name for you. Now create your own chop in one of the following ways:

> Cut a 1"–2" square or rectangular piece of Styrofoam from a meat package and draw your characters onto it using a pencil or sharpened stick. Be sure to reverse the pattern so it will print correctly. Using red printer's ink and a brayer, cover the Styrofoam and place it face down on the artwork to be "signed." Roll over it with a clean brayer or carefully turn the work over and rub gently behind the chop.

> Form a piece of clay by pinching it into the desired shape—dragon, lion, swirls, etc. Be certain to keep the base of the clay flat by pressing it against the table. Trim the edges of the base until it forms a square shape (some chops are round). When the clay has set, but is not completely dry, scrape out your character design on the flat bottom. Allow to dry completely, then fire.

> Use the method described above with cooked dough or salt clay, or try carving a potato, carrot, or soap. Print with printer's ink, red tempera, or a red stamp pad.

Make a Chinese Scroll Book

Look at examples of Chinese painting until you feel at one with the lifeforce, or Chi, of the style! Select a paper suitable for watercolor and cut it lengthwise into 6" strips. Overlap and glue the strips end to end until they reach the desired length. Fold the strip accordion-fashion so that each square measures 4-1/2" x 6" or so. In pencil, lightly sketch on your scroll a long continuous scene in the Chinese style; then draw over your pencil lines with India ink. When the ink is dry, dilute more ink in water to form a "wash" and paint a misty shading on your piece. You may also choose to add a little watercolor in special places for emphasis, but be sure to keep it very light and subtle.

Cut out two rectangles that measure 5" x 6-1/2" or 1/2" larger on each side than your folded scroll. Using Chinese print, cover material such as wallpaper, marbleized paper, or fabric, cut out two more rectangles that measure 7" x 8-1/2". Trace around the cardboard rectangles on the back of the covering and trim each corner diagonally. Wrap the cover around the cardboard and glue the edges down. Glue the folded scroll over the edges. Sign your work with your chop.

chop

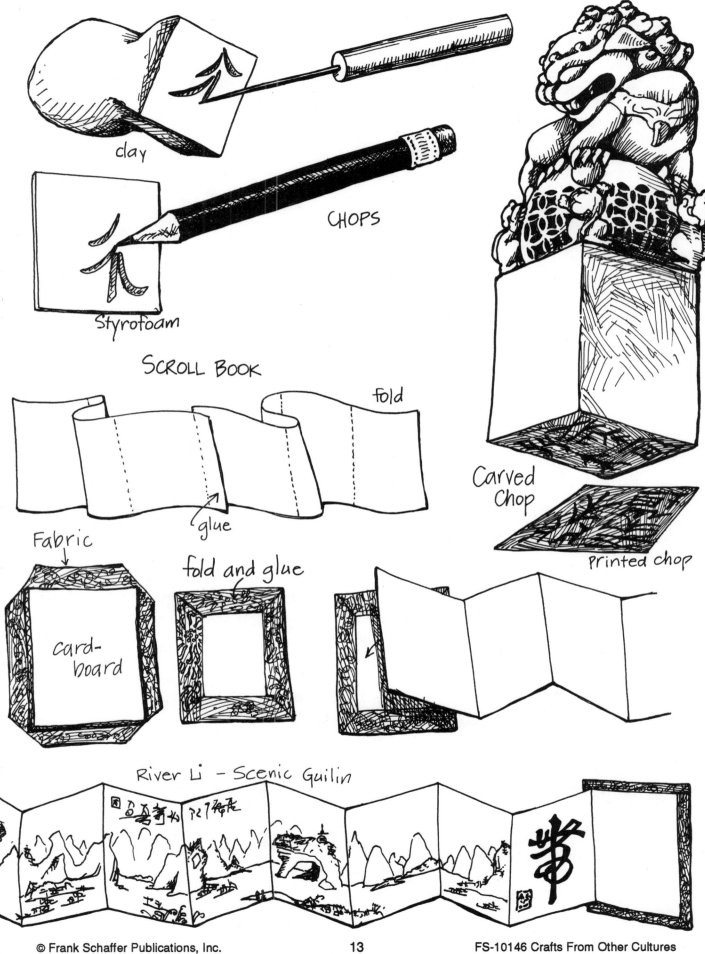

clay

CHOPS

Styrofoam

SCROLL BOOK

fold

glue

Fabric

fold and glue

card-board

Carved Chop

printed chop

River Li – Scenic Guilin

Shadow Puppets

Shadow puppets are made in many far eastern countries, and China is no exception. They are generally well-known legendary figures and, like Chinese traditional opera, they relate old and loved stories. The puppets themselves are constructed of thin, stiff, translucent animal hide, dyed and intricately cut. The arms, legs, hands, and heads are made separately and tied on so they move independently; then each part is attached to a long stick. The puppets are held up to a white sheet with a light shining behind it so that a colored shadow appears on the sheet. The puppeteer manipulates the puppets by moving the sticks.

In a puppet show you will see not only puppets of people, but also of horses, tigers, mythical animals, and even great palaces complete with thrones constructed by using the same technique.

Activities and Projects

Puppet Show

Design some shadow puppets or use these figures of the last emperor of the Tang Dynasty and his favorite concubine, Yang Guifei (said to be responsible for his downfall).

Plan your puppet on paper and, using a fine-lined permanent marker, transfer your design to translucent plastic cut from a gallon milk carton or from the base of a bacon wrapper. Place the plastic over the drawing and trace all the details. Color in areas with permanent colored markers; then cut out each piece and all the inner details. Use heavy thread to fasten on the arms and legs and attach 1/4" dowels to the body parts as shown in the illustration. Practice moving your puppet.

Use oaktag to make the characters of your favorite children's story. Be certain to add lots of cut out inside details since oaktag is opaque. Glue the finished puppets on sticks and give the kindergartners a show.

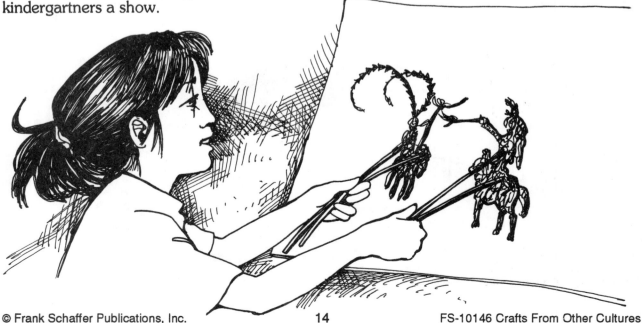

Heavy lines show separate pieces.

Dots show points of attachment.

Fine lines show cut out portions within pieces

Chinese New Year and the Dragons

Probably the best-known Chinese festival in the United States is the Chinese New Year. It falls soon after our own New Year on a floating date and is the cause of great festivities among the Chinese.

The end of the old year is a time for settling all old business and starting fresh. It is also a time for "spring cleaning." Everyone should have all new clothes from inside out so demons will not recognize them in the new year. Children especially love this holiday because they are given "Lucky Money" in red envelopes by all the grownups. Great feasts are held, many firecrackers are exploded through the night and day, and the Dragon Dance takes place.

Dragons are considered benevolent by the Chinese, not frightening or evil as in some folklore. The dragon represents strength, wisdom, and the spirit of change. The Chinese call themselves "children of the dragon." A dragon is said to have the head of a camel, the horns of a deer, the eyes of a rabbit, the ears of a cow, the neck of a snake, the belly of a frog, the scales of a carp, the palm of a tiger, and the claws of a hawk. It is also said to have a beard and whiskers and is deaf.

The Dragon Dance occurs on New Year's Day. Chinese spend months creating a huge head with ears that wiggle, eyes that light, and a mouth that opens. A long cloth body is added. Each new dragon is given an "eye opening" ceremony before its first parade. The dragon is manned by specially trained dancers, who practice until they can perform the ritual steps perfectly and keep the dragon moving during the parade. A masked Buddha leads the dragon to exploding firecrackers and large bowls of lettuce with red envelopes filled with "Lucky Money" set out by shopkeepers. The dragon devours the food, then spits it out, keeping the money and bringing luck to the shop.

Activities and Projects

Build a Chinese New Year Dragon

Begin with a sturdy cardboard box to serve as an armature for the head of the dragon. Crumple up balls of newspaper to form the eyes and other desired lumps and bumps, and twist rolls to form brows, nostrils, and lips. Tape these features in place with just enough masking tape to secure them; then layer the entire head with long strips of newspaper dipped in thin wallpaper paste. Pinch, press, and add additional wads of newspaper until a dragon's head eventually emerges. A final layer of recycled paper towels will make it easier to mark for painting. Allow the head to dry completely; then paint in outrageously bright colors of tempera or, if the dragon is to be used outside and may get wet, use acrylic or latex enamel in accent colors. Paint an additional piece of cardboard for the lower jaw and attach it to the underside of the head with staples or a hot glue gun. Glue on bits of gold and silver foil or anything shiny. Sew or staple old sheets together end to end to form the body. Fashion a "spine" down the center by attaching garlands such as those used for party decorations or Christmas tree trimming. Cut out scraps of colored paper, foil, wrapping paper, tissue paper, and cloth and staple to the sheet for scales. Perform a Dragon Dance on Chinese New Year. Gung Hay Fat Choy! (Happy New Year!)

horn

eyes

nostrils

brows

Crumpled and twisted newspaper

Cardboard box

lower jaw

oaktag ears

gym hoops for structure

(inside view)

Crepe paper streamers for beard

Chinese Symbols and the Zodiac

The ancient Chinese astrologers felt that events on earth repeated themselves every 12 years or so and that people born in a particular year all seemed to possess similar character traits. An animal whose traits best matched those of the people was selected for each of the 12 years in the cycle and the Chinese Zodiac was born.

The 12 animals selected are the rat, the ox, the tiger, the rabbit, the dragon, the snake, the horse, the sheep, the monkey, the rooster, the dog, and the boar. Remember the Chinese idea of these animals' character traits is not necessarily the same as ours in the West. For example, in the West the pig (boar) is considered to be lazy and dirty, while the Chinese consider the pig hard-working, hospitable, and trusting.

The Chinese believe that a person must be careful when his or her year comes around every 12 years. For example, dragons must be careful in the Year of the Dragon. The year can be very lucky or very unlucky.

Not only do the 12 animals of the zodiac symbolize character traits, but many other animals, flowers, and objects are symbols, also. The bat represents happiness; the peach—longevity. The lotus is a symbol of purity and perfection. It is a symbol of Buddha. Buddhism was born when Prince Siddhartha went in search of a means to alleviate people's misery. He became Buddha and is often seen sitting on the lotus because, just as the beautiful lotus rises out of the mud of slimy ponds, so did his teachings arise out of the suffering of the world.

Many designs recur in Chinese arts and crafts. Most of these are highly stylized symbols that the Chinese recognize and understand. On the next page are some common designs that appear on temples, palaces, tapestries, rugs, porcelain, and art. Their origin may be Taoist or Buddist, but they are no longer connected with any religion; they are representative of the national Chinese culture.

Activities and Projects

Design a Zodiac

Use the symbols shown on the next page to design your own Chinese zodiac. Divide a large circular piece of paper into 12 wedges (a compass does this easily with no measuring) and place one animal of the zodiac in each wedge. Draw the animals and various other elements of the zodiac on separate sheets of colored paper and assemble them onto the large circle. This method will create more contrast and prevent the whole calendar being ruined by one small mistake. Be sure to include some of the traditional Chinese motifs on borders and draw the animals in a Chinese style, not necessarily realistically. Include the character traits and years of each animal so that you can tell people about their traits. You can determine years not given by adding or subtracting 12 from those which are listed.

Remember to use lots of red because the Chinese love that color. When Chinese kindergartners draw pictures in school they always make the sun red instead of yellow as we do in this country. They think we are silly to even ask why. "Because the sun *is red!*" they say.

Cloud Symbols

Fire Symbols

Five bats surrounding "Shou" (longevity)
Symbolizes five great blessings:
Happiness, Wealth, Peace, Virtue, Longevity

Pearl Border

Cloud Border

Still Water Border

Sea Waves and Sea Spray

The Art of Chinese Cooking

Cooking and eating are very important in China. Mealtime is not merely for eating; it is a time for people to enjoy one another's company. Chinese people believe a good meal should be a balance of crunchy and soft foods, spicy and mild, sweet and sour, hot and cold. Many dishes are served at one meal and everyone takes a little of each from the center of the table with their chopsticks.

Because fuel for cooking is expensive and food prepared on the streets is cheap and plentiful, many Chinese eat out. Some streets in China are filled with one small stall after another offering delicious tidbits. There are usually a few tables by each stall where people can sit, or the food is nibbled while they wander around chatting and enjoying the outdoors.

The Chinese often create exotic dishes with exotic names. One such dish is called, "Dragons Playing With Pearls." It consists of black bumpy strips of sea cucumber (the dragons) in a rich brown sauce with small hard-boiled quail eggs (the pearls). Peking duck is perhaps the most famous delicacy. If you order duck in Beijing, you will first be served duck tongue soup, then crispy-fried livers and gizzards. Finally the duck will be presented at your table. It has been specially fed and fattened, roasted over sweet fruitwood to absorb the aroma, and glazed with malt sugar to make the skin crispy and brown. The chef will carve it into small pieces to be rolled up in a flour tortilla-like pancake with sauce and green onions.

Another very popular food in China is dumplings, or won ton. They are stuffed with one of many fillings, folded in a variety of configurations, and cooked by several methods, but they are all delicious. The following is one easy recipe:

Mix together: 3/4 lb. ground pork or sausage
2 tablespoons grated fresh gingerroot
2 tablespoons Chinese wine or sherry
1 tablespoon sesame oil
1/2 - 1 cup finely minced carrots, celery, green onion, water chestnuts, etc.
salt and pepper to taste

Cook an olive-sized portion of the filling and taste it to check the seasonings. Refrigerate the mixture until ready to use. Drop 1/2 teaspoon of the filling into the center of a wonton skin and fold and seal the edges as shown. Repeat with the rest of the filling. Place on cookie sheets until ready to cook. In a saucepan, bring two 10-ounce cans of chicken stock (add water) to a boil. Add the wonton or six at a time and cook about three or four minutes until filling and skin are done. Remove with a slotted spoon. Repeat until all wonton are cooked. Add a little cold water (1 ounce) occasionally after dropping each batch of wonton to cool the stock and slow cooking.

Wonton are delicious served with soy sauce, plum sauce (mix a little soy in plum or apricot jam), or hot chinese mustard. Put small saucers of each in the center of the table. Wonton are also good in chicken soup made by adding a tablespoon of Chinese wine or sherry, a sprinkling of sesame oil, and a few sliced mushrooms and green onions. Leftovers can be fried in a hot skillet with a little oil until they are crispy, then sprinkled with ginger soy. This may be the best way of all to eat wonton!

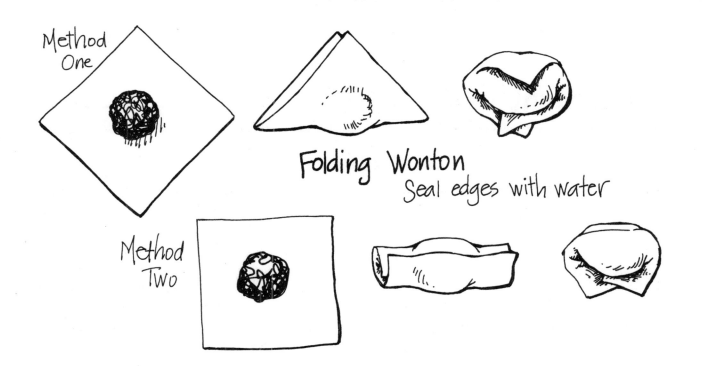

Method One

Folding Wonton

Seal edges with water

Method Two

Using chopsticks

First chopstick held stable
Second chopstick held like pencil
Chopsticks held in the middle for balance

Tips together

Incidentally, the Chinese fortune cookie is unknown in China. It was invented by the Chinese who came to the west coast of the United States!

Bibliography

Burling, Judith and Arthur Hart. *Chinese Art*. New York, 1953.

Glubok, Shirley. *The Art of China*. New York, 1973.

Jia, Qi. *Terra Cotta Warriors and Horses of Emperor Qin Shi Huang*, Hong Kong: Man Hai Language Publications, 1987.

Malloy, Ruth Loy. *Fielding's People's Republic of China 1991*. New York: William Morrow and Co., 1991.

Ming Shu. *The Art and Practice of Chinese Astrology*. Hong Kong: Darwell Import Co. Inc., 1991.

National Geographic Society. *Journey Into China*. Washington, D.C., 1982.

Sormani, Giuseppe, ed. *The World and Its Peoples—China I and II*. New York: Greystone Press, 1965.

India

India's culture is a result of all the varied peoples who have made India their home throughout history. Beginning as far back as 2500 B.C. with the Dravidians and the Indus in 1500 B.C., the Moghuls, the Portuguese, and finally the British, India has grown to absorb the best of these cultures to produce a rich and wonderful culture that is uniquely its own. The same is true of the art of India. Each successive culture that came to India brought, along with its beliefs, its crafts and arts to blend with the already rich traditions. The result is a wide variety of art objects decorated with the sumptuous ornamentation loved by Indians and the rest of the world.

FS-10146 Crafts From Other Cultures

The Indus Valley Civilization

The Indus Valley civilization is one of the oldest on earth, dating as far back as 4000 B.C. In 1922 artifacts were unearthed which led to the discovery of two ancient cities, Harappa and Mohenjo-Daro, which thrived between 2500 B.C. and 1500 B.C.

These cities were very advanced—planned and arranged on a grid pattern, with shops, restaurants, granaries, drainage systems, and two-story homes enclosing inner courtyards. Archeological digs suggest a society with an intricate writing system that has not, as of yet, been deciphered. Farmers cultivated wheat, barley, fruit, and cotton. A wealthy merchant class traded cotton, timber, ivory, copper, gold, and precious stones with other cities of the Middle East.

The arts were also highly developed in the Indus Valley. Statues have been discovered of mother goddesses and other deities, indicating that these earliest people were close to the earth, worshiping natural objects and other earth forces. Many examples of intricately decorated wheel-turned pottery have been unearthed, as well as cast bronze tools and figurines, terra-cotta animal whistles, toys, and soapstone stamps carved with elephants, tigers, antelopes, bulls, and other animals who lived in that region. The stamps also bear inscriptions in a pictographic-type of writing, so they are thought to have been used to stamp packages for shipping, but no one knows for certain.

Copper "Dancing Girl" from Mohenjo-daro

Activities and Projects

Examine the stamps shown below that have been excavated from Mohenjodaro to discover the artistic style of these ancient craftsmen; then design a stamp of your own in a similar style.

First sketch your design on lightweight paper in the actual size. The original stamps were quite small, measuring 1" to 2" across. Next, speculate about the use and meaning of the stamps and decide the purpose of your stamp. If you feel the stamps were signatures, like Chinese chops, you may wish to select an animal whose attributes symbolize the strengths of your family, and create your name in "Indus Valley" pictographs. You may wish to design a stamp to show you are shipping a load of cotton or even computers! Use terra cotta clay to pinch-form a stamp shape that is easy to grasp with a flat base large enough to fit your sketch. When clay is leather-hard, or stiff but still wet in appearance, transfer your sketch onto the base of the stamp by laying the paper over the base and lightly pressing over all the lines. Be certain the stamp is the reverse of the desired finished product so it will print the correct image. Remove the paper and carefully carve the details of your stamp with small knives and carving tools. Allow to dry completely and fire.

Use the stamp on fresh clay pieces to "sign" them, or ink them with printer's ink and print onto paper or fabric.

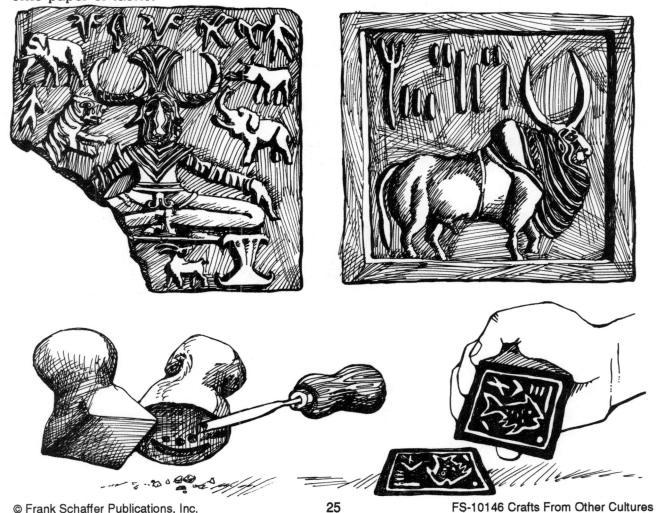

Hinduism

In 1500 B.C. India was invaded by the Aryans, a wandering tribe of herders who dominated it for 1,000 years and left behind an important body of sacred literature called *the Vedas*. The Vedas tell us how Indians believed the universe originated, rules for living, prayers and rituals, and heroic epic adventures with moral lessons. These writings, combined with some Dravidian gods and goddesses, are the basis for Hinduism.

More than 80 percent of Indians are Hindus. Three major elements of the Hindu faith are *dharma*, or moral duty, *karma*, or reward and punishment for good and bad deeds, and *reincarnation*. The religion recognizes one god, Brahman, whose complexity cannot be understood by man unless broken up into many gods. These gods increase and decline in popularity as time passes. Currently the most popular are Brahma, the creator, Vishnu, the preserver of life, and Shiva, the destroyer. These gods can appear in many forms. Krishna is one incarnation of Vishnu. He is very handsome, strong, brave, clever, and well-loved. He appears often in Hindu art as a blue figure playing the flute.

Most Hindus worship these gods at small shrines in a corner of their homes, but there are also Hindu temples, which are massive and ornately carved with sculptures depicting episodes from the lives of the many gods. Hindus make pilgrimages to these temples where they circumnavigate the sacred shrine. Stalls are set up to sell incense, small idols, and flowers to leave as offerings, as well as trinkets, jewelry, and novelties. There is singing and dancing and people camp nearby, cooking over small fires. The atmosphere is very festive.

Holidays in India are also festive. "Diwali" is celebrated for five days in the fall in honor of the Hindu god Lakshmi, the giver of wealth. "Holi" celebrates the downfall of the evil demoness Holika; everyone wears old clothes and throws brightly colored powder on one another as they meet in the street. It is a time when wives may insult their husbands, and servants their masters. During "Durgha Punja" large papier mache images of the goddess Durgha are worshiped for a week in the center of the village, then floated downstream.

Vishnu

Krishna

Shiva

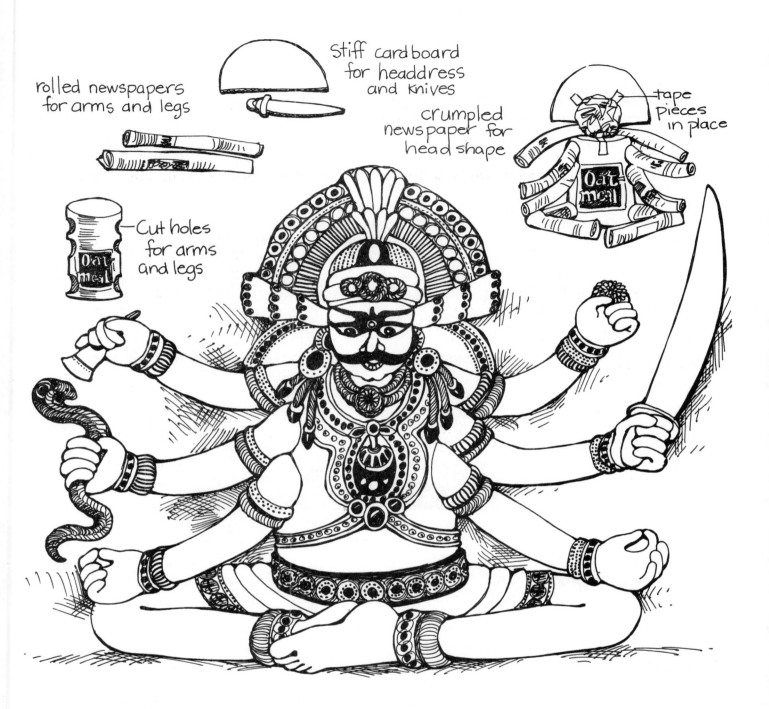

rolled newspapers for arms and legs

Stiff cardboard for headdress and knives

crumpled newspaper for head shape

tape pieces in place

Cut holes for arms and legs

Oat meal

Activities and Projects

Create an imaginary figure similar to the gods and goddesses from the Vedas. Write a fantastic story about your character's brave and heroic deeds. Begin with sketches, then using a discarded cardboard container such as an oatmeal box as the base, build up legs, arms, facial features, and headdresses with newspaper papier-mache. Add a final layer of recycled paper towels for a smooth even finish and allow to dry completely. Paint your sculpture with tempera or acrylics, and decorate with shiny facrics, foil bits, plastic beads, and sequins.

Hindu Music and Dance

Vedic literature is the basis for many art forms in India. Classical Indian dance began with the Vedic priests who moved their hands as they chanted their prayers. These movements gradually evolved into precise, stylized gestures of the entire body, including the fingers, hands, legs, feet, and even the face and eyes. Training for classical dance begins in the temples at an early age. Often dancers teach their skills to their youngsters throughout childhood. Most often the dancer acts out an episode from Vedic literature with the dancer playing all the characters in the story. The dancer may make a ferocious face to portray the buffalo-headed demon Mahishasura, or flutter the eyelids flirtatiously to portray Satyabhama, the beautiful maiden Krishna favors. Hand movements may appear almost like sign language as the dancer motions the words to a love song such as Jayadeva's "Gita Govinda."

The dancer is a sight to behold—covered with gold, flowers, and silk. Painting the fingertips and soles of the feet scarlet and wearing jangling anklets and bracelets help to accentuate the movements.

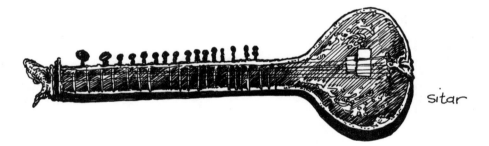

sitar

Activities and Projects

Design and construct a classical Indian dancer doll. Begin by twisting wire to form an armature in the desired size and dancing shape. Using newspaper strips and thin wallpaper paste, gradually build up the form. Add details by crunching balls and twists of paper and taping them in place with the moistened newspaper strips. When satisfied with your work, add a final layer or two of recycled paper towels, smooth all the edges, and allow to dry completely.

Use tempera or acrylics to paint the parts of the figure that will be visible. Emphasize the eyes and add red to the fingertips, palms, toes, and soles.

Using a bright colored lamé, taffeta, or silk fabric, fashion the costume. Then glue on bits of gold or silver aluminum foil, plastic beads, sequins, and other sparkles.

Glue the figure to a painted wooden base so it appears to be in mid-step.

wire armature

clay figure

paint on
blouse

folds

Elephants

Elephants are very important in all aspects of Indian culture. In the southern peninsula, they roam wild through the forests. They are used as beasts of burden in the jungles because they are able to navigate through dense foliage where there are no roads for motor vehicles. During festivals and holidays, they are elaborately decorated and paraded through the streets.

An ancient Hindu myth tells the story of the first elephants, who were said to have wings and play among the clouds. One day a holy man was teaching his pupils under a tree when a group of elephants lit on one of the branches and broke it. They squashed some of the pupils and infuriated the holy man, who called on the gods to remove their wings. Now wingless and earthbound, the elephants remained friendly with their former companions, the clouds, and could still call upon them to bring much-needed rain to ensure a good harvest, which brought prosperity.

The elephant appears among the pantheon of Hindu gods in the form of Ganesha, the elephant-headed god who brings prosperity to those who worship him.

GANESHA

Elephants appear in all shapes and sizes in Indian art. Among the largest are those carved in granite as part of the *Descent of the Ganges*, a sculpture from the seventh century in Mahamallapurah, south of Madras. Children delight in the tiny flat carved ivory elephants no larger than 1/8" across which fill a hollow red seed with a tiny ivory cork so they do not escape. In every size between these two extremes are elephants of ivory, teak, terra cotta, papier mache, and brass. They are also found in the motifs printed on many fabrics.

Activities and Projects

1. Carve an "ivory" elephant from a large bar of soap. Begin by sketching front and side views of your elephant; then scratch the outline on one flat side of the soap with a sharp stick or pencil. Then carefully carve away the excess with a pocket knife or paring knife. Save the scraps to wash your hands!

2. Expert carvers may want to try the same project in wood.

3. Using any colored moldable substance such as cooked dough, salt clay tinted with food coloring (see recipe on page 4), or oil-base clay, form an elephant as shown below. While the clay is still soft, press in tiny beads, sequins, and bits of plastic for decoration, and allow to dry completely. Use glue to refasten any decorations that become loose once the project has dried.

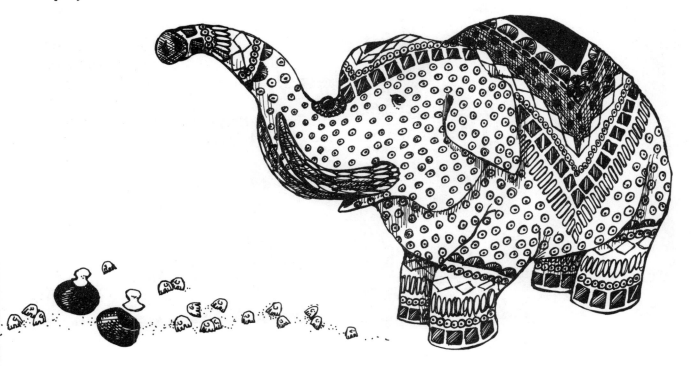

Muslims and the Taj Mahal

In 1526, the Muslim king Babar invaded India, and so began the Moghul Empire period of Indian history. Babar's grandson Akbar was the greatest Moghul ruler because he recognized the great diversity of the Indian people and worked with that diversity instead of trying to destroy it. He encouraged artists and poets of all faiths to be creative.

Shah Jahan, a successor in the line of Moghul Emperors, was responsible for building that monument which has come to symbolize India to the rest of the world—the Taj Mahal. When his beautiful and beloved wife died during childbirth in 1631, he was so heartbroken that he ordered the Taj built for her mausoleum. It took 21 years (until 1653), but the result was a brilliant blend of Hindu and Muslim styles. The design is basically a Muslim mosque based on Islam concepts, but the use of native materials and the decorative motifs were all Hindu. The construction required 20,000 craftsmen and laborers from India, Asia, and even Europe.

The building is made entirely from white marble inlaid with precious stones. Shah Jahan originally planned to build a similar mosque for himself out of black marble across the river from the Taj Mahal, connected by a silver bridge, but he died before it could be built so he and his wife are buried together inside the Taj.

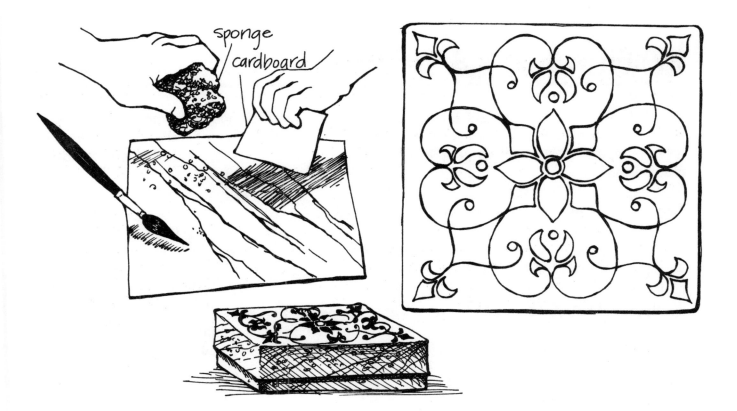

Activities and Projects

Many of the art forms in India involve inlay. Furniture is carved and often inlaid with mother-of-pearl, wood, brass, or stones. Small stone boxes are common in markets all over the world.

Make your own *faux marbe* (fake marble) inlaid box. Begin with a small jewelry box with a lid. Trace around the lid and sketch a design of flowers in a style similar to those created by the craftsmen who built the Taj Mahal. Make two copies of your sketch.

Assemble several colors of papers whose surfaces are printed to resemble marble. These may be purchased, or create your own. Marble effects can be created by using a sponge to apply acrylic paints sparingly to a base sheet of heavy paper. Then add streaks in the "stone" by drawing an edge of cardboard through the wet paint. Use fine brushes to add additional streaks of contrasting shades. Dab the edges slightly with a sponge so they are not all sharp.

When the papers dry, cut pieces to cover the base and the lid of the box (as shown). Place the lid design over the lid paper and carefully cut out all the flowers through both papers with an exacto knife. Glue the lid and the base papers to the box with a thin coat of white glue. Use the copy of the design to cut out each individual flower, stem, and leaf from a contrasting piece of marbleized paper, and glue each into its place. Securely glue all corners and edges. When the box is completely dry, apply several coats of decoupage, polyurethane, or other sealant.

Indian Weddings

In India, most marriages are still arranged. Parents feel that their age and experience enable them to choose someone with similar background and values for their child so the marriage is more compatible. Most young people agree that this is a good system, though there are love matches also.

Weddings are most festive occasions that may last for days and cost a great deal of money. All Indian parents, rich or poor, are expected to finance lavish spreads for friends and relatives, and to provide dowries for their daughters, even though the Dowry Prohibition Act of 1961 forbids them. Many Indians begin saving when their daughters are born.

The actual wedding ceremony is long and takes place amidst a backdrop of flowered screens and other decorations. The bride is elaborately dressed in a sari of red or pink which symbolizes love and happiness. She is covered with gold, pearls, and flowers. Her hands and feet are decorated by her female relatives with intricate lace patterns painted on with mehindi paste (henna dye) that will last for weeks and tell everyone she is a newlywed.

Activities and Projects ——————————————————————

Decorate your own hands. Using a fine point marker, illustrate your hands and/or feet, or persuade a friend to volunteer. Study the example shown here, and then design an original in the same style. If this custom seems strange to you, think about tattoos!

Appliqued Felt Rugs From Kashmir

In the northernmost section of India lies the beautiful land known as Kashmir. With the jagged snow-covered Himalaya Mountains all around, the vale of Kashmir grows fruit on its lush slopes. In the center of the vale, the Dal Lake is a popular summer spot where tourists live in houseboats. Many people of Kashmir have blue eyes, which are highly unusual among the rest of the nation's population.

Kashmiris produce some of the finest handicrafts in India, including boxes and other articles from enameled papier mache, hand carved walnut furniture, soft woolen shawls, and appliqued felt rugs.

Activities and Projects

Make an appliqued felt rug or wall hanging. Felt is simply wool fibers that have been deliberately tangled and shrunk. Begin with raw wool that has been picked clean of weeds and rinsed in tepid water and a little gentle soap. Some farmers who raise sheep might be willing to give or sell you a small portion of a fleece, or you may contact a spinner or weaver. Select two pieces of old cloth such as sheeting that is several inches larger in all directions than the finished piece will be. Spread the wool evenly over one sheet about 3" to 4" thick and cover it with the other sheet. Fold and baste all four edges and also baste the sides together at about 1" intervals so that it holds together securely. Wash the piece vigorously in detergent and hot water, squeezing and agitating the fibers. This heat and motion causes them to become tangled and matted together and is called "felting." Rinse thoroughly and peek at one corner to make certain the wool has felted. Repeat the procedure if necessary. Lay flat and cover with a heavy board or cookie sheet with books or bricks on it to weight it down and leave it overnight. Allow to dry completely.

Cut a piece of paper the size of the finished felt and plan your design and color scheme. Use wool thread in a chain stitch to embroider it onto the felt.

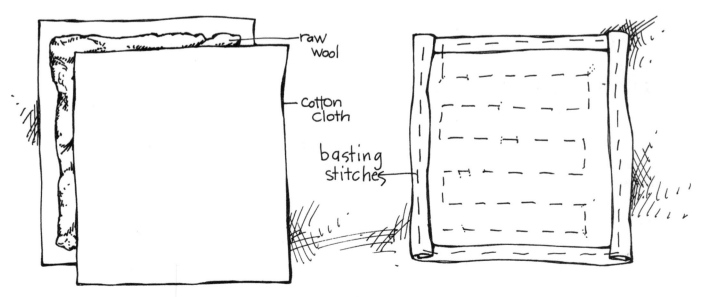

raw wool

cotton cloth

basting stitches

Chain Stitch

1.

2.

3.

4.

For an interesting variation, add some raw wool that has been dyed between the two sheets of cloth, or add some wool yarn in a border or design. It is difficult to tell exactly how the wool and thread will tangle into the finished felt, so the result is imprecise, but beautiful.

Cotton and Silk Production, Clothing

In India, as in China, colors have meaning—red is the color of love, yellow symbolizes spring. Pink means welcome and orange represents the earth. Blue is the color of Krishna, of clouds, and of rain.

The Indian people love ornamentation and brilliant colors, as is evident in the beautiful silk and cotton cloth they produce and export throughout the world. Export began late in the seventeenth century when printed cotton cloth called *chintz*, which means "spotted cloth" in Hindi, made a sensation in Europe. India's dying techniques were far superior to Europe's at the time, and the Indians' interpretations of English, Dutch, and French designs seemed wildly exotic to Europeans. Intricate patterns of animals, plants, and geometric designs are block-printed by hand on cotton cloth in factories and cottage industries for saris, bedspreads, and yard goods. Silk is woven and embroidered with silver or gold threads for special occasions.

In India, most women wear saris, a rectangular piece of cloth six yards long which is wrapped around and folded various ways. Some women wear long shirts or loose-fitting pants that are tight at the bottom. Many men wear the traditional garb adopted by Mahatma Ghandi called the "longhi." And, like elsewhere in the world, many men, women, and children wear western-style clothes.

Activities and Projects

Try your hand at block printing by creating a small tablecloth or throw pillow. Study the examples of traditional designs shown here to discover how they repeat. Sketch a design of your own using the same style elements and determine how many repeats are necessary to produce the desired finished size. Color your sketch in as many colors as you plan to use on your print. Make several copies of your design. Transfer and carve your design from a wood or linoleum block; remember it will print the reverse of what you see. Cut away those portions of the design which show the background color, and leave intact the parts that are to print. Make a separate block for each color. Try out the finished blocks on a scrap of cloth to see that everything lines up. Prepare your cloth by making certain it is clean and free of sizing and wrinkles and that it lies flat on a smooth, padded surface. Using permanent printing ink for cloth, print one color at a time, allowing each inking to dry before doing another. Follow the specific instructions on the ink label to set the color in your fabric properly.

Make a simplified version of the previous project on paper, using water soluble printers' ink and Styrofoam (from meat packaging) for printing blocks.

Indian Cooking

Indian cooking varies greatly throughout this vast nation. Each region has its specialties depending on what foods are abundant there. In the north where wheat is grown, wheat breads called *naan, puris,* and *chapatis* are common, while in the south, rice is favored. Hindus are vegetarian for the most part, Muslims do not eat pork, but curries are eaten everywhere. A curry is a stew-like dish seasoned with many aromatic and wonderful spices. The main ingredients may be vegetables, meats, poultry, fish, or eggs, and each household has its own favorite combination of spices, called *masalas,* which are ground fresh each day.

Activities and Projects

Explore the art of Indian cooking.

Chicken Curry
- 4 chicken breasts (cut into chunks)
- 3 t. salt
- 1/4 c. oil
- 1-1/2 c. chopped onions
- 1 T. minced garlic
- 1-1/2 t. minced ginger root
- 1 t. each ground cumin, tumeric, ground coriander, red pepper
- 1-15 oz. can peeled tomatoes (chopped)
- 1/2 cup plain yogurt
- 1/4 t. each: cinnamon, cardamom, cloves, black pepper
- 1/4 c. peas, raisins, cashews (optional)
- 1 T. lemon juice

garlic

ginger root

Score chicken chunks, rub with salt, fry in oil in deep skillet for three to four minutes, until meat becomes firm and white, but not brown. Transfer chicken to plate and add onions, garlic, and ginger to the oil. Fry seven to eight minutes, add spices, then tomatoes, yogurt, peas, raisins, cashews, and the chicken. Simmer for 20 minutes until chicken is cooked. Sprinkle with lemon juice and serve with rice and/or chapatis.

Meals are served on large brass trays with small portions of several curries, rice, and condiments and pickle. Indian pickle is not like our sweet or dill pickles. It is made from pieces of lime, green mangos, vegetables, or tiny shrimps preserved in oil and lots of hot spices. Only a small quantity is needed to add a burst of flavor. Sometimes instead of trays or plates, meals are served on large, freshly cut banana leaves, making clean-up very convenient! Generally no utensils are used to eat other than the fingers of the right hand. The left hand must remain in the lap.

Special desserts are often decorated with shiny silver leaf. This is available in thin sheets and looks like aluminum foil, but you need not remove it—it has no taste and it is edible!

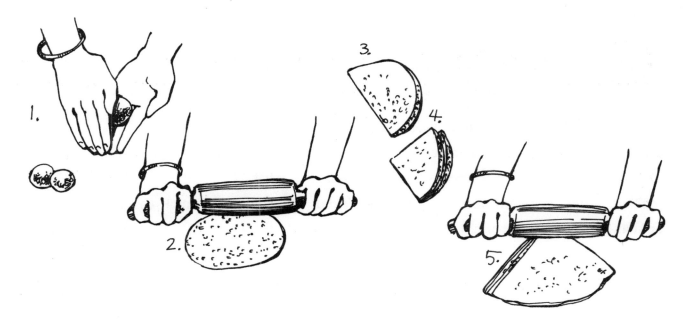

Try making some chapatis to eat with your curry. In a large bowl, mix 1 c. whole wheat flour, 1 c. white flour, and 1 t. salt. Make a well in the center and add 1 c. warm water. Stir by hand in a circular motion gradually mixing in all the flour until a stiff dough is formed. Knead the dough into a ball, adding a bit more flour or water if necessary. Divide dough into walnut-sized balls and roll flat on a lightly floured surface. Spread a thin layer of butter (called *ghee* in India) and fold in half. Spread more butter on the half and fold again, forming a triangle shape. Roll out the chapati a final time so that it is as thin as possible and fry until crispy and brown on both sides in a skillet or griddle sprinkled with a few drops of vegetable oil.

41

Bibliography

Brown, Joe David. *India*. New York: Time Incorporated, 1961.

Library of Nations–India. Amsterdam: Time-Life Books, 1986.

Lye, Keigh. *Take a Trip to India*. London: Franklin Watts Ltd., 1982.

McNair, Sylvia. *Enchantment of the World–India*. Chicago: Childrens Press, 1990.

Schulberg, Lucille. *Historic India*. New York: Time-Life Books, 1968.

Mexico

In the capital of Mexico, Mexico City, lies La Plaza de Tres Culturas (The Plaza of Three Cultures). In this one area stands the ruins of an Aztec temple, a Spanish church, and a modern steel and glass skyscraper. These three structures are representative of the three major periods in Mexico's history—the pre-Columbian era with the advanced Indian civilizations such as the Olmecs, the Mayans, and the Aztecs; the Spanish colonial era; and the modern, post-revolutionary era. As different as these three eras seem, they are tied together through the art and folk art of the people—modern Mexican muralists incorporate ancient Indian styles and symbols into their work, Spanish Catholic saints took on characteristics of favorite Aztec gods, and Mexican folkartists today use both Indian and Spanish art for inspiration to produce items that are famous around the world. Underlying all Mexican art is a love of bright, beautiful colors and a strong sense of form.

Ancient Indian Civilizations

Olmec head

Although it is thought that human beings wandered in the land that is now Mexico as long ago as 40,000 B.C., the first major civilization, the Olmecs, did not begin until around 1200 B.C. Their surviving art gives us clues to the lives they led. They worshiped a god whom they believed took the shape of the jaguar and created fine jade jewelry of human figures with jaguar heads. They are also known for their massive stone heads, some of which are 9 feet high and weigh over 40 tons. They developed the first calendar based on an advanced knowledge of astronomy. Succeeding peoples of the Mexican region were influenced by the Olmec civilization.

The Mayans improved upon the Olmec calendar and also developed an advanced form of hieroglyphics to record birth dates, succession of rulers, and famous battles. Enough carved stone examples have been unearthed to determine that the Mayans had a writing system with at least 800 different signs. At gravesites, archeologists have also uncovered many miniature figurines made from clay in the form of gods, goddesses, men, women, children, and animals. Though small, they are elaborately decorated with beads, feathers, jewelry, masks, capes, and tattoos, and they show traces of the bright paint. Interestingly, many of them were whistles and rattles, perhaps used ceremoniously.

Mayan hieroglyphs

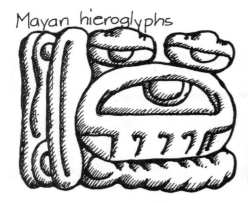

Activities and Projects

Make a Mayan clay whistle. Study the examples of Mayan figurines shown here to acquaint yourself with the style used by the ancient Mayans. On a sheet of paper sketch a design of your own in the Mayan style. Draw your design from the front and the side. Add head-dresses, necklaces, skin textures, or any other creative form of ornamentation. With a small ball of clay (2"–3" diameter) use the pinch method to fashion a hollow form in the general shape of your design, leaving one end open, like a balloon, through which to blow. Insert a flat wooden stick (Popsicle stick) into the hole and out again nearby. Trim around the two holes. Allow the whistle to harden slightly before adding all the details. Attach limbs by roughing up the surface with a sharp point (scoring) and "gluing" them on with slip (clay mixed with water to the consistency of thick cream). When the whistle is leather-hard (rigid but still appears wet) test it by blowing gently through the hole making sure the second hole is not covered. Use a sharp needle to clear the hole if it is blocked. You can vary the notes the whistle will make by adding a few more holes and covering first one, then another.

Fire your whistle in a kiln, paint or glaze it, and blow it!

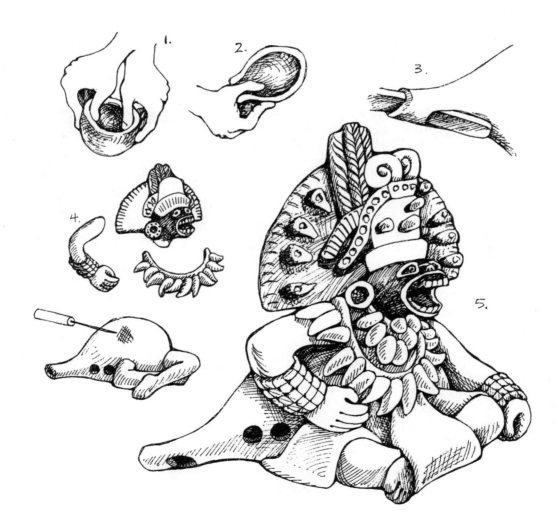

Mayan Weaving on Backstrap Looms

The Mayans developed weaving into a high art form which is still practiced by a few modern-day Mayan descendants. The Mexican government encourages Indians to keep these and other traditional crafts alive through a body called the Institution Nacional de Indigenismo (National Indian Institute). It has established museums to display the Indians' beautiful work and assist them in selling it to tourists and other national agencies.

The geometric designs are formed with combinations of stripes, rectangles, chevrons, and triangles in age-old patterns. Red, white, black, gray, yellow, and blues were used, but today more colors are available.

Just as their ancient ancestors did, today's Mayans use backstrap looms. The weaver ties one end of the loom around her hips, and the other around a tree or post. She then kneels in front of the tree, keeping the proper tension on the threads by varying her distance from it.

Activities and Projects

Make a belt on a backstrap loom. Measure your waist, add 48" and cut 12 pieces of sturdy yarn or string that length. Line up the strings and tie one end of the bundle firmly to an 18" ruler or stick. Using heavy cardboard or mat board measuring 2" x 4", cut 6 slits and 6 holes 1/4" apart and thread a string through each one. Straighten all the threads and tie the other ends to another ruler. Use a 4"–6" wide strap of old cloth to tie to each end of the ruler and around your hips. Use another piece of cloth at the other end to go around a tree, post, table leg, or doorknob. Sit at a distance from the tree so that the strings are taut. Pull up the cardboard guide and insert a pencil 6"–8" from the ruler. Lower it and insert another pencil. These will keep the weaving straight and will be removed later. Study the traditional Indian patterns and begin weaving. Create stripes by changing colors, diamonds by increasing one color and decreasing another. You may pull the guide up and down as you weave, but sometimes you may find it necessary to thread a pattern through by hand. As your weaving grows, move closer to the tree while winding it onto the ruler and retie the strap around your hips. When you have about 12" of string left on both ends, finish your belt by braiding the strings together and knotting the ends.

Lace your backstrap weaving through the belt loops of your favorite jeans and tie it up!

Spanish Invasion

Hernando Cortes arrived in Mexico in 1519 looking for gold. The country would never be the same again. The Spanish easily defeated the Indians because they had iron armor, guns, and horses which did not exist in the New World. They also had legend on their side. Aztecs believed that their feathered serpent god, Quetzalcoatl, who left Mexico (heading east), would return in the year of One Reed by the Aztec calendar. Some said the god was bearded, pale-skinned, and hated human sacrifice, which was demanded by another Aztec god, Huitzilopochtli. Cortes seemed to fit the legend perfectly so Montezuma, the Aztec ruler, thought Cortes was the feathered serpent god, Quetzalcoatl, and was afraid. By the time the Aztecs figured out that the Spanish were merely men after their gold and riches, it was too late.

Quetzalcoatl

The Indians did not fare well. Two-thirds of the population were slaughtered or died of small-pox and other diseases the Spanish brought with them. Aztec priests were persecuted and books were burned, destroying 3,000 years of knowledge. But many of the Indian beliefs and customs became incorporated into those brought by the Spanish. During fiestas (celebrations of various religious holidays) held today, many costumes and dances are featured which the ancient Aztecs and Mayans would recognize.

One such festival is called Las Posadas, held during the nine days before Christmas in remembrance of Mary and Joseph's journey to Bethlehem. Children travel from house to house carrying their *naciniemto* (nativity scene) and singing songs. When the procession is over, the children break a *piñata*. The piñata is a papier-mache animal filled with candy, trinkets, and toys which is hung from the ceiling. Children are blindfolded and take turns whacking it with a stick until it breaks and out fall the treasures hidden within.

Activities and Projects

Make your own piñata. Begin by blowing up a balloon roughly the same shape as the animal or object you intend to create. Using 1" wide newspaper strips coated with wallpaper paste, build up the body around the balloon. Leave a small hole through which to add the goodies. Use crumpled newspaper to add appendages and details and secure them in place with more strips. Allow the piñata to dry completely, add the candy, then seal the hole and cover the entire surface by gluing on brightly colored tissue paper in fringes. Use your imagination to add finishing touches such as eyes, ears, tails, or spots with bits of foil, sparkles, or colored paper.

newspaper

paper towel layer

The Marketplace

Mexico has several major cities. Five of the larger ones are Mexico City, Guadalajara, Monterrey, Puebla, and Cuidada Juarez. These cities share many of the problems and opportunities of large cities everywhere, but the majority of Mexicans live in small villages. Whether these villages are very poor or reasonably comfortable, they all have two things in common—a plaza and a marketplace. The central plazas are a Spanish tradition. They are usually paved with stones, shaded with trees and surrounded by government buildings and the main town church. Sometimes there is a bandstand in the center for the bands who play during the many fiestas.

The marketplace lies nearby, sometimes in a large covered warehouse. The market is comprised of many small one-person stands. Farmers come to sell fruits, vegetables, meats, chickens, and dairy products. T-shirts, herbal medicines, pottery, bottled beverages, brooms, craft items, fast food, and everything else you can think of are also available. Markets have been going strong since the days of the Aztecs.

Activities and Projects

Create a market day diorama. Many Mexican folk artists create whimsical figures from wood, clay, cloth, and any other materials on hand. Use your own imagination to make a tiny, bustling market day scene. Begin with a sturdy plain cardboard box and cut the sides down to measure 4" - 5" high. Study photographs of Mexican markets for the necessary details. Spread a little dirt or sand on the floor. Dress clothespins in serapes and embroidered blouses. Add yarn braids or use salt clay tinted with food coloring, tempera, or acrylic to form sombreros, fruits and vegetables, and other items for sale. Make vegetable crates from Popsicle sticks or balsa wood. Add a few animals and some crying babies and some T-shirts imported from the United States with logos of rock groups. Add baskets, crates, pots, and some palm trees for shade with construction-paper leaves. The more items you add, the more you will think of to add. Make everything very bright and colorful.

Next, try making a diorama of a fiesta in the town plaza.

Text visible within the illustration:
PARA PURIFICAR LA SANGRE
PARA EL SISTEMA NERVIOSO
PARA LOS NERVIOSO FALTA DE SUEÑO

FS-10146 Crafts From Other Cultures

Terra Cotta Tiles and Lanterns

Many Indian villages are famous for their fine craftsmanship of one particular craft such as silver jewelry or baskets. Puebla, to the south and east of Mexico City, is known throughout the world for its beautiful blue and white tile.

Terra cotta tile is used for many purposes in Mexico. Architect Juan O'Gorman covered an entire building in tiles to form a mosaic Indian scene. Tile walls are beautiful, colorful, and long lasting. Tile floors are cool to walk on in the heat of summer.

Activities and Projects

Make a lantern using terra cotta. Decide what size and shape your lantern will be and cut a pattern from heavy paper. You will want it large enough so that a free-standing candle will fit comfortably inside. Study the designs shown and sketch one of your own in a similar style onto your paper pattern.

Using the slab method, roll out some clay (like cookie dough) about 1/4" thick until it is large enough for your pattern. To achieve an even thickness, place a ruler on each side of the clay. Lay the pattern over the clay, cut around the edges and mark the design by punching holes with a sharp stick or pencil. Remove the pattern and cut the holes with a plastic straw or sharp knife. Join the two edges and smooth with a knife while the clay is still pliable. Allow finished lantern to dry completely, glaze it or leave it natural, and fire it in a kiln.

Make a lantern using tin. Use the same procedure as above for the pattern, then lay it on a piece of tin flashing. Place the flashing on an old piece of wood and secure it with a nail in two or three places. Using a hammer and nail, pound holes through the pattern and flashing as your pattern shows. Remove the tin from the board and cut out your lantern with tin snips, and hammer a shallow fold into each end and attach the ends by the folds.

Make an assortment of lanterns in different sizes and designs. Light a candle in each one and wait until dark!

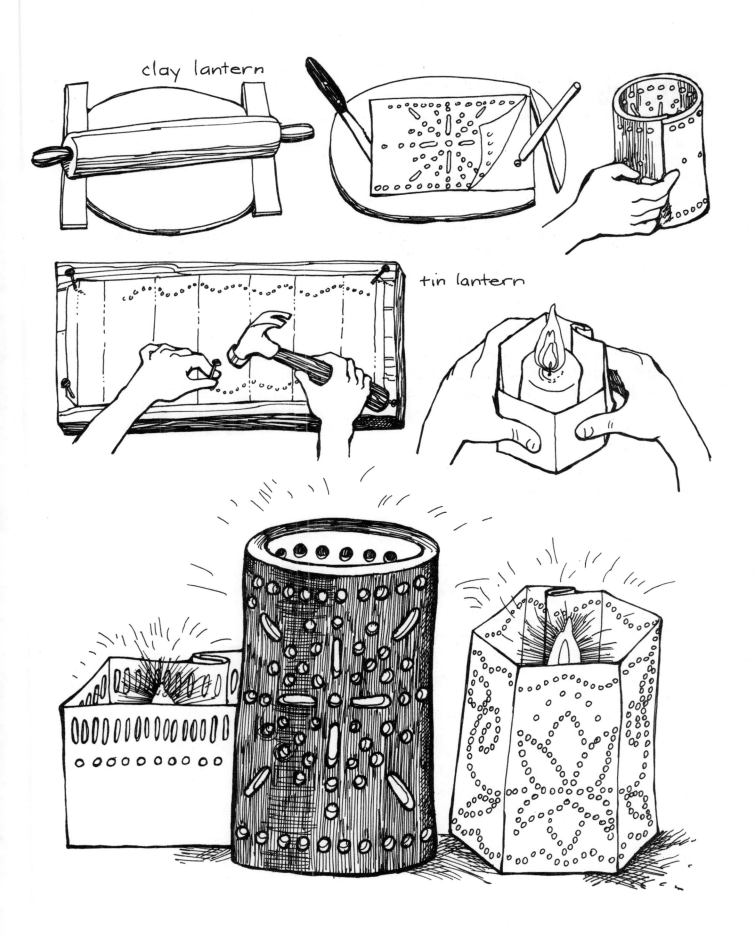

clay lantern

tin lantern

FS-10146 Crafts From Other Cultures

Flowers

The Mexican people love bright colors. Many homes painted in reds, yellows, blues, and oranges seem even more vibrant against the sunny blue sky. Flowers of all kinds grow wild in the Oaxaca Valley and elsewhere and are also planted in pots and gardens and lovingly tended. These beautiful flowers also appear embroidered on the white cotton blouses worn by young girls and women. The art of embroidering and the traditional designs are handed down from generation to generation. Blouses and other embroidered items are popular among tourists.

Activities and Projects

Make a Mexican embroidered blouse. Study the pattern shown here and make a pattern on newspaper, adjusting the pieces according to your own body measurements. Using light-weight white cotton, cut out the pieces. Now embroider the yoke in a flower design drawn lightly onto the fabric with pencil. Use many colors of embroidery floss. Now sew the pieces of the blouse together and gather the sleeves with a drawstring of braided embroidery floss. The finished blouse will look great with blue jeans and cowboy boots!

For an easier project, embroider flowers on a store-bought blouse, a T-shirt, a canvas book or beach bag, or a handkerchief.

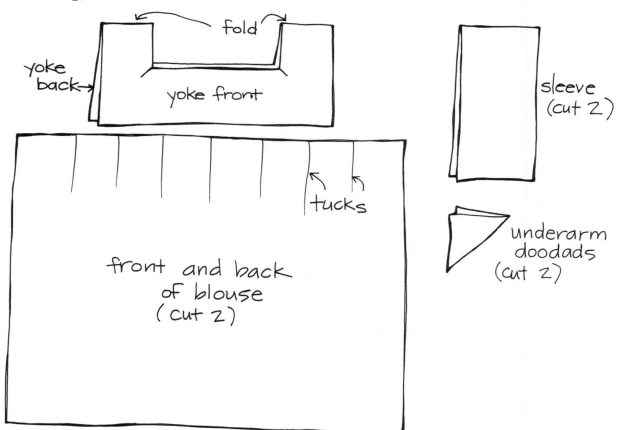

The Sacred Paper of San Pablito

From pre-Columbian times, Mexican Indians have considered paper to have a religious meaning, using it for sacred writings and ceremonial dress. Though the Indians in the tiny village of San Pablito have long embraced Spanish Catholicism, they still have a reverence for the special paper they produce, using much the same technique they have all these centuries. The paper is made from the inner bark of fig trees, which is boiled in limewater to soften it. The fibers are then laid out in a grid pattern on a smooth surface and pounded with a flat stone until they spread out into a sheet which is sun-dried and trimmed.

The paper is in such demand by artists that the whole community works hard to produce enough to sell, but some of the paper is always kept back to make religious books and cut-out paper figures.

NACIMIENTO DEL NIÑO JESUS.

The books contain well-known scenes from the Bible such as "Nacimiento del Niño Jesus" (the nativity) shown here, or spirit figures, cut from darker handmade paper or brightly colored commercially produced tissue paper. Sometimes the papercuts represent evil spirits and are burned in a special ceremony to dispel those spirits.

Activities and Projects

Cut out some paper spirit figures. Create your own spirit figures by folding brightly colored tissue paper in half and snipping out monstrous shapes. Use Quetzalcoatl or other ancient Indian gods for your inspiration. If possible, select natural-colored, rough paper that appears handmade, which may be available in art supply stores, or use newsprint or textured wallpaper samples. Glue the figures onto paper with thinned white glue or rubber cement. Make up a myth to accompany your figures and carefully write it on the page as the Shamans of San Pablito do.

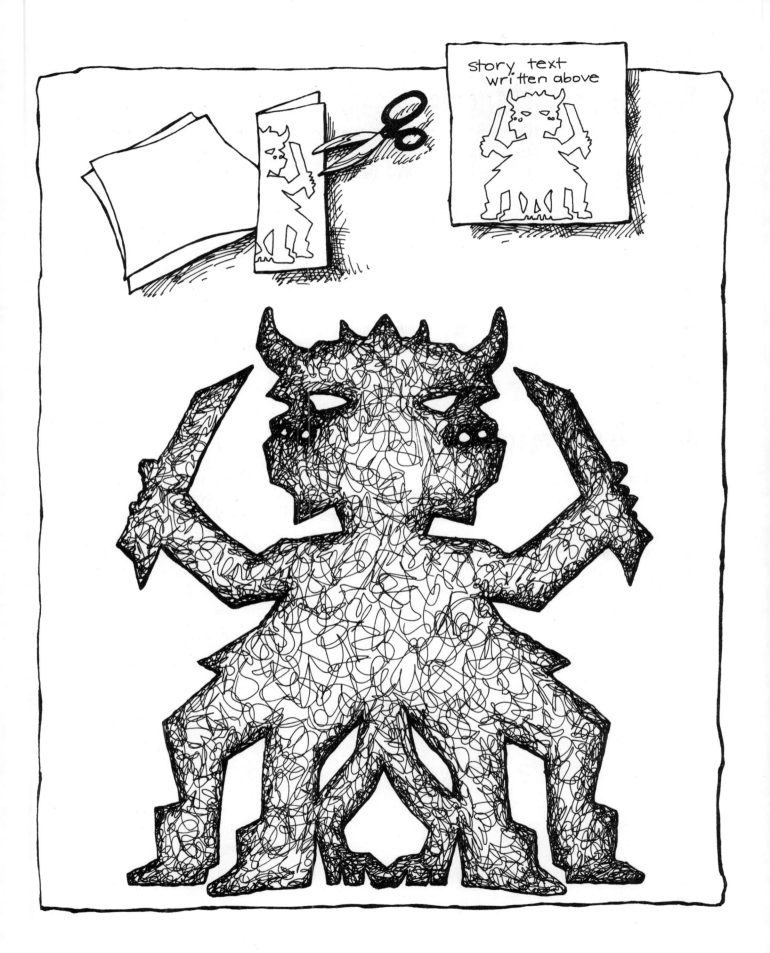

Modern-Day Murals

The 1920s and 1930s have come to be known as the Mexican Renaissance in art and literature. Sparked by the political upheaval of the times, writers produced work which truly reflected peasant life and revolutionary fighting. Artists began doing the same on a large scale—murals. One muralist, José Clemente Orozco, stated, "The highest form of painting, the purest, the strongest, is the mural. It cannot be turned into an object for personal profit; it cannot be hidden for the benefit of the privileged few. It is for the people. It is for all."

The mural was not new to Mexicans. The ancient Mayans and Aztecs created huge and powerful stone carvings and frescos, and Spanish churches and shrines were also adorned with frescos. The modern muralists, such as Diego Rivera, combined pre-Columbian images such as the jaguar and the feathered serpent with Spanish religious skeletons and added revolutionary generals and villains for good measure. He was a huge, flamboyant figure whose energy seemed unlimited and whose work often offended people, but he remains one of the major forces responsible for the direction of art in Mexico today.

Activities and Projects

Paint your own mural. Look for a suitable wall or use a large sheet of paper on a bulletin board. Study Mexican art from one of the three major periods of its history—pre-Columbian, Spanish colonial, or post-revolutionary. Design a mural to fit your space in your favorite style or include images from all three. When you have finalized the design and colors, enlarge the design using an opaque projector, an overhead projector (you will need a transparent Xerox), or the grid system. Divide the sketch into squares and the wall into the same number of squares, only larger. Then carefully redraw the sketch, square for square. Though frescos are traditionally painted on fresh plaster so that the paint becomes one with the wall, you can use tempera paint (if your work is temporary) or acrylic paint for greater permanence. Quarts of latex enamel wall paint cover a great deal of area, last a long time, clean up easily with soap and water, and can be purchased in accent colors. Black, white, yellow, magenta, and turquoise can be blended to create any shade.

Pacal, Son of
Chan-Bahlum,
Mayan ruler from
A.D. 615-683

Mexican Cooking

When the Spaniards arrived in Mexico they were introduced to many strange foods. Some of them were decidedly unpalatable to Spanish tastes such as dog, winged ants, waterfly eggs, corn smut (this item may be making a comeback), and dried algae, but many others are enjoyed today by people all over the world. They are known by their ancient Indian names— tomatoes, avocados, squash, chilies, turkeys, beans, maize, and chocolate. Chocolate was valued so highly by the Aztecs it was sometimes used for money. They also enjoyed drinking hot cocoa made with red hot chilies!

Maize, or corn, is the staple of almost all Mexicans' diets. Whatever else is eaten, each meal is accompanied by tortillas. Many Mexicans who live in the city buy ready-made tortillas and heat them at home, but many, especially villagers, prefer them prepared the traditional way. This requires that the corn be soaked in caustic limewater overnight to soften it. Then it is ground with grinding stones called *mano* and *metate* so that it has that special "taste of the stone." The ground dough is then pounded into round flat shapes and fried on a hot griddle.

Chicken Mole (Mole-ay) is a favorite Mexican dish featuring a rich sauce made with chocolate. Each household has its own secret recipe which it passes down from generation to generation.

Try this recipe for Chicken Mole:

> 3 whole chicken breasts (deboned and cut in pieces)
> 3 T. oil
> 1 medium onion, chopped
> 3 garlic cloves, minced
> 2 T. flour
> 1 green pepper or equal amount of your favorite pepper
> 4 T. toasted sesame seeds
> 1/2 t. cinnamon
> 1/4 c. each almonds and pine nuts (or all almonds)
> 2 slices of bread, dried and crumbled (or 2 tortillas)
> 1 can peeled tomatoes (14-16 oz.)
> 1 can chicken broth plus 1 can water
> Salt and pepper
> 2 oz. semi-sweet chocolate, chopped

Heat oil in heavy dutch oven. Add chicken and fry until firm and white, not brown. Remove chicken, add onions and fry until soft. Add garlic and flour. Fry two minutes, then return chicken (and juices) to pan. In a blender or food processor, combine pepper, sesame seeds, cinnamon, almonds, red pepper, bread, and tomatoes and blend until smooth. Add blender mixture and chicken broth to chicken, bring to a boil, reduce to lowest heat, cover, and simmer for two to three hours. Add chocolate, salt and pepper to taste and serve immediately with plenty of tortillas!

metate and mano

Bibliography

Carrasco, David and Eduardo Matos Moctezuma. *Moctezuma's Mexico.* CO: University Press of Colorado, 1992.

Casagrande, Louis B. and Sylvia A. Johnson. *Focus on Mexico.* Minneapolis: Lerner Publications Co., 1986.

Constable, George, ed. *Library of Nations—Mexico.* Time-Life Books, Inc., 1985.

Josephy, Alvin M., *The American Heritage Book of Indians.* American Heritage Publishing Co., Ltd., 1961.

Lye, Keith, *Take a Trip to Mexico.* London: Franklin Watts Ltd., 1982.

Smith, Bradley, *Mexico—A History in Art.* Garden City, NY: Gemini-Smith, Inc., 1968.

Stein, R. Conrad, *Enchantment of the World—Mexico.* Chicago: Regensteiner Publishing Enterprises, Inc., 1984.

Wood, Tim, *The Aztecs.* New York: Viking Penguin, 1992.

The story of Russia can be learned from examining its art. Primitive rock pictures found in the northern region tell us that 3,000 years ago people lived there who wore furs, hunted, and were familiar with the sea. These early Slavs were pagans and constructed large obelisks, some nine feet tall, as idols. They were overrun by wave after wave of invaders from the East. The first of these invaders were the Scythians who settled, then invaded Greek cities to the south and brought back golden objects as part of their booty. In the ninth century, the Varangians, Scandinavian brothers to the Vikings, began to invade, trade, settle, and rule over the Slavs. Vladimir, who ruled from Kiev from A.D. 980 to 1015, was so impressed with Byzantium that he adopted its Christianity for all his people. Icons of the Russian Orthodox Church remain as perhaps Russia's most important art form.

Because Russia is so vast, spreading through Europe and Asia, Russian art has been influenced by both continents. Most recent art, called *Socialist Realism* reflects the political climate. Only paintings glorifying the state have been allowed. With the breakup of the Soviet Union, however, new paths are opening up. It will be interesting to see which directions art forms take as they reflect this new freedom of the Russian people.

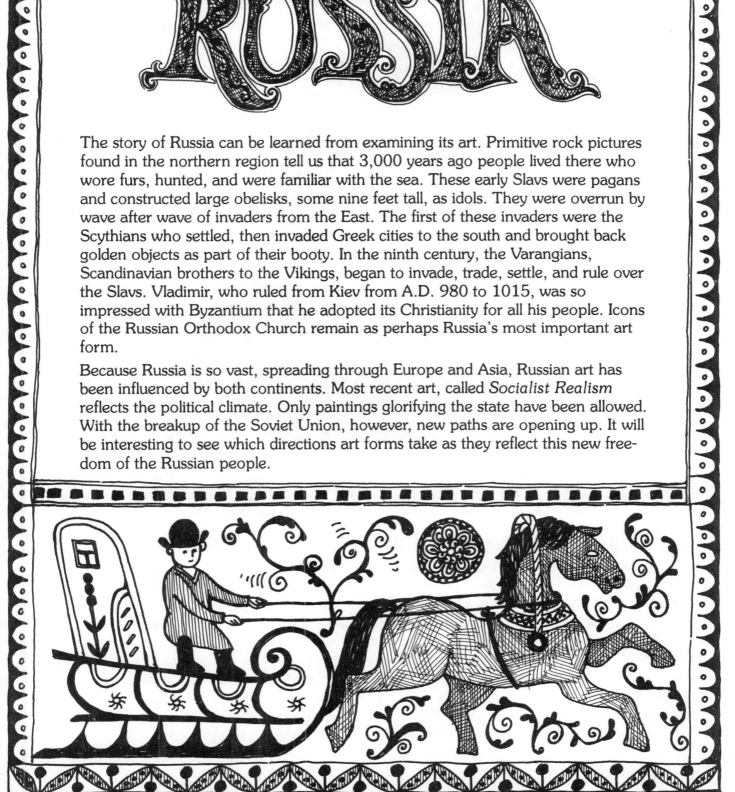

Icons

From the tenth until the early sixteenth century, Russian art was expressed mainly through icons. *Icons* are small paintings of religious subjects such as Christ, the Virgin Mary, or saints and angels on wooden panels. The artists, usually anonymous, did not strive for originality, but painted in the time-honored tradition according to the rules set down in a book called the *Podlinnik*. Because icons focus on the spiritual rather than the physical, they are stylized rather than realistic, with stiff lines and gilt backgrounds. The figures themselves are painted in rich, vibrant colors. The paints and brushes used to create the icons were blessed, and the finished work was consecrated by priests. As a result, icons were said to possess powers to cure illness and to protect against invaders. The icon shown above, called *Our Lade of Vladimir*, is thought to have saved Moscow from foreign armies three times. Icons can be found in every Orthodox Church and every home—from palaces to peasants' huts. They reflect the strong Christian faith of the people of old Russia.

Activities and Projects

Make a Russian icon. Study the details and style of the sample icons shown; then sketch one of your own on a sheet of paper the same size as your plank of wood (5" x 7" x 1" is a good size). Lay the sketch over the wood and trace it, pressing hard enough so that small grooves appear in the wood. Spray the wood with gold paint; then paint the figures with acrylics or enamels in rich colors. Paint the large areas first, then details such as the facial features. When paint is completely dry, rub on a thin coat of brown shoe polish and buff most of it off again so that the grooves retain the dark color. This will make it appear centuries old! Protect your work with a light coat of spray varnish.

Mosaics

Mosaics were another art form that came to early Russia from Byzantium. Like painted icons, mosaics reflected the stiff spiritual style, golden background, and the beautiful vibrant colors of the Byzantines. Mosaics were formed with tiny bits of glass, stone, and tiles. As the Russians adopted these art forms, they began to change them somewhat. Though they remained religious in meaning, sometimes the figures were Slavic in appearance and dressed as famous warriors.

Activities and Projects

Create a mosaic. Collect a supply of glass and ceramic tiles. Stained glass artists usually have pieces too small for their own use, and tile companies may have odds and ends left over from jobs or discontinued tiles. Break the tiles into irregular pieces approximately 1/4" x 1/4". Taking into account the quantity of tiles you have collected, cut a piece of 1/4" plywood or paneling as a base for your mosaic and glue wood strips (painted laths or wooden yardsticks) around it to make a shallow box. Create a design that will work with the colors you have. You may want to work in the style of Byzantium or create a style of your own using a floral pattern such as those that appear so often in other Russian folk art. Since your finished piece will not have lines to separate areas, be certain to select colors that contrast. Keep your design simple, as small details are difficult to show with this art form. A good method to use to plan your mosaic is to cover a piece of cardboard with masking tape, sticky side out, and lay the tile pieces onto it just as you will on the finished product. You can then easily rearrange any areas until you are completely satisfied with your design. Glue the pieces onto the plywood just as you have planned and allow to dry completely. The surface of the tile pieces should be as near level as possible. Apply grout (used to tile bathrooms) over the entire surface, work it into the spaces between the tile pieces and remove excess with a rubber spatula or straight piece of cardboard. Use a damp sponge to gently wipe the mosaic immediately so that tiles show through and the wooden edges are clean, and then wipe it again after the grout has dried.

sketch

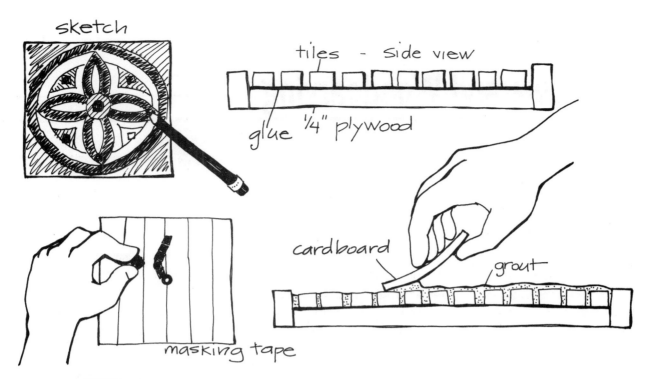

tiles - side view

glue ¼" plywood

cardboard

grout

masking tape

FS-10146 Crafts From Other Cultures

Windows and Woodcarving

Perhaps because wood was readily available from the vast stretches of forest that grow across Russia, or because it provided warmth as well as shelter in Russia's harsh climate, people in Russia have always preferred to build in wood. Instead of saying they would build a town, they said they intended to "cut" a town because of the wooden logs they cut and shaped with axes to construct their homes. The Church of the Transfiguration on Kizhi Island in northern Russia is an excellent example of the great skill of Russian craftsmen. The entire structure, with its 22 domes, was constructed without blueprints, surveying tools, or even nails!

Russian carpenters used the same skill to create their homes. Even the smallest peasant home was built tight with notched logs, then holes were cut out for the windows and doors. Then woodcarving skills and creativity came into play as shutters for each window were fashioned of wood in elaborate and very beautiful designs. Some are painted many colors, some are a solid color base with white lacy "gingerbread," and some are left unpainted to weather naturally.

The Russian carpenters filled their homes with wooden furniture and made many household objects from distaffs for spinning, to bowls, mugs, and even imaginative birdhouses like the ones shown here. (The birds enter through the nose of the man and the mouth of the woman.)

trace

cut

sketch   mat board or balsa

photo back   cardboard

Activities and Projects

Make a Russian window picture frame. Study the examples shown here; then plan one of your own in the same style on a sheet of paper cut to the desired finished size of the frame. Since the window will be symmetrical, you can fold your paper in half and trace it onto the other side. You will need a stiff material for your frame such as heavy cardboard or mat board. Framing shops will sometimes save scraps when they become too small for mats. Balsa wood used for model building also works. Trace the outline of your design onto the back of your board and carefully cut it out with a sharp utility knife or an exacto knife. Use a metal straightedge to cut the center square. If you are planning to paint your frame a solid color, do it at this point using spray enamel, enamel, or acrylic. Now cut out the swirls, diamonds, and other shapes of your design. Paint them and carefully glue them into place with a tiny amount of wood glue. When your frame has dried completely, position your favorite picture from the front, then tape it to the back with masking tape. Glue a picture hanger or the ends of a small piece of string to the top of the frame for hanging. If you want to set your frame on a desk, cut a piece of cardboard about 2" wide and 9" long. Score, fold, and glue it onto the back of the frame as shown.

Babushkas and Bread Dough

When we hear the term *babushka*, we think of the scarf tied around the head of an older women, usually from Russia, but in Russia the term is used affectionately to mean "grandmother." Babushkas (wearing their *babushkas*) play an important role in Russia. Many live with their children and take care of the house, the shopping (which often means standing in long lines), and they care for their grandchildren so that both parents can work.

The floral and animal motifs found on embroidered babushkas (scarves) are also embroidered on aprons, tablecloths, and traditional costumes. They are the same motifs as those painted on wooden plates, mugs, and boxes, and those carved on shutters and furnishings.

Sometimes these motifs are formed from bread dough. Small intricately twisted loaves called *kalachi* are a favorite snack of the people.

Activities and Projects

Russians sometimes use ingenious sculptures formed from bread dough as decorations on their kitchen walls. Make a bread dough sculpture with Russian motifs. Study some of the traditional woodcarving motifs shown here. Then sketch some designs of your own in a similar style. Thaw ready-made frozen bread dough and let it begin to rise, then punch it down and form it into the shape you have designed. Remember the dough will plump up somewhat during baking. Using scissors and sharp knives, cut textures, small balls, and worm-like shapes for hair, eyes, or flower petals. Beat an egg with a tablespoon of water to stick on details. When your sculpture is complete, gently brush the egg wash onto the entire surface and bake according to the directions until it is nicely browned. Cool the sculpture completely, then apply several coats of spray-on varnish to the front and back to completely seal it. Glue a small wire or colorful ribbon to the top to hang it.

These decorations make excellent gifts for your babushkas!

roll

snip

poke

snip

score

St. Basil's Cathedral

Perhaps the most recognizable landmark in Russia is St. Basil's Cathedral located in Moscow's Red Square (the word for "red" and "beautiful" are the same in Russian). St. Basil's was constructed in 1555 by Ivan the Terrible to celebrate his victory over the Tartars. It consists of nine unique domed chapels, eight surrounding a central dome. Though built in stone, it was modeled after similar designs in wood. Ivan thought the finished church was the most enchanting work he had ever seen. He summoned the two Russian architects responsible and congratulated them on a job well done. Then he ordered that they be blinded so they could never again create anything as magnificent!

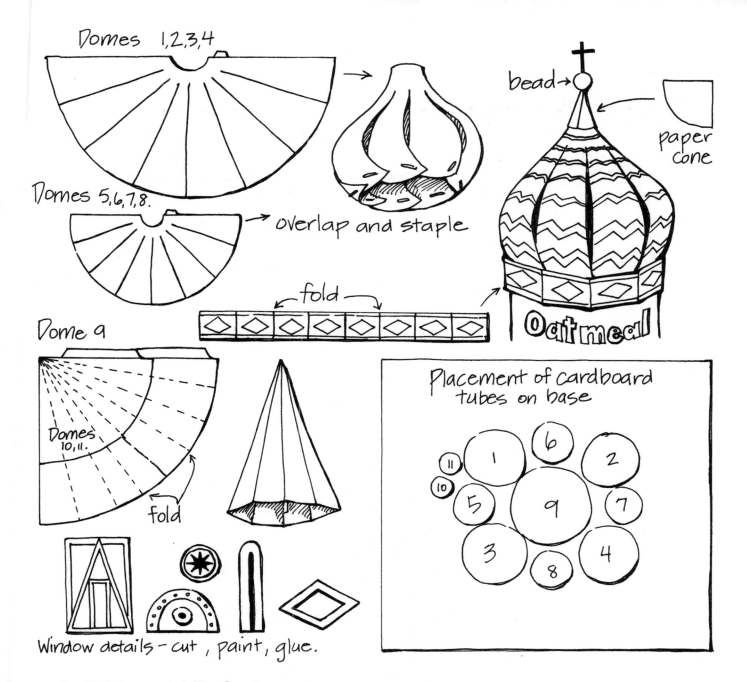

Domes 1,2,3,4

Domes 5,6,7,8.

overlap and staple

bead→

paper cone

fold

Dome 9

Oatmeal

Dome 9

Domes 10,11.

fold

Placement of cardboard tubes on base

11
10
1
6
2
5
9
7
3
8
4

Window details – cut, paint, glue.

Activities and Projects

Make a scale model of St. Basil's. Collect cardboard rolls of various sizes and some sheets of cardboard of similar weight, such as the back of a paper pad or oaktag. Construct each of the nine domes separately according to the illustration. Use a hot glue gun or white glue to attach the various parts. Assemble the church on a sturdy cardboard or plywood base with eight domes surrounding the ninth like an eight-pointed star. When the glue is completely dry, paint the details, referring to a colored photograph. Paint the base white. As a final touch, sprinkle the domes and base with transparent glitter to represent snow—Russia is a cold place much of the year.

The Bolshoi Ballet

The Russian people have had a passion for ballet since the eighteenth century when Catherine the Great brought it to Russia. There are over 40 major dance companies flourishing in the nation, but the Bolshoi ballet is the most famous. Each year the ballet school accepts only about 35 of the hundreds of promising children who apply. Once accepted, the students study ballet as well as their regular school courses for nine years, and then they may try out for the Bolshoi ballet, which accepts only the best of the best. Russian ballet owes much of its popularity to Peter Ilyich Tchaikovsky (1840–1893), who wrote three of the most famous ballets in the world—*Swan Lake, Sleeping Beauty,* and *The Nutcracker.* Each year at Christmas time Americans flock to see this famous ballet which is staged all over the country.

Activities and Projects

Each dance company that stages *The Nutcracker* adds its own personal creativity to the designs of the characters' costumes and the stage settings. Now it is your turn. Use the basic ballet figures drawn here and design paper dolls with costumes of the various characters in the ballet such as—the Sugarplum Fairy, the Chinese Dancers, the Snow Queen, the Toy Soldiers, the Mice, and the Nutcracker himself.

Listen to Tchaikovsky's music while you are working so you will be in the proper mood!

Eggs, Eggs, and Eggs

Long before Christianity, pagans decorated eggs to symbolize the sun's life-giving forces, fertility, and the rebirth of spring. Now Christians decorate eggs at Easter to symbolize spiritual rebirth. Russians decorate eggs made of wood nested one inside another, each more intricately designed than the last. (Nested dolls are a popular and well-known Russian folk art, too.) Beautiful Ukrainian eggs, called *pysanky*, are made each year with wax and dyes in delicate patterns according to tradition.

Peter Carl Fabergé (1846–1920) gained great fame for the exquisite jeweled eggs that he made for the Russian royalty. He made over 50 different eggs in all before he went into exile in 1917.

Fabergé Egg

Nested Eggs

Pysanky Egg

Activities and Projects

Create a "faux" (false) Fabergé egg. Begin with a blank egg shape. Use a wooden egg purchased from a craft store, a plastic egg left over from Easter or pantyhose packaging, or a hard-boiled egg that is free from cracks and is at room temperature. Assemble assorted beads, sequins, embroidered ribbons, metallic fabrics, anything shiny. Take a moment to examine the eggs shown here and also your supply of "jewels." Sketch a rough idea of your egg on paper first and then lightly mark the surface of your egg according to your sketch. Using a hot glue gun or white glue, carefully decorate your egg according to your design. You may find it easier to place small pieces onto your egg with tweezers. Glue small lids and bottle caps together to form a base so the egg will not roll when it is finished. Do not forget to decorate the base as well.

Chess

The Russian people have enjoyed the intellectual challenge of the game of chess since the tenth century. All over Russia, city parks like Gorky Park in Moscow have permanent chess boards set up and people gather there on summer evenings to play or watch. It is considered a sport and the spectators are eager to watch the championships every year.

Activities and Projects

Make your own chessboard and pieces. Begin by sanding a board that measures at least 12" x 12" until it is smooth. Leave a 2" border around the entire board and divide the remaining 8" x 8" square into 1" squares by marking it lightly with a pencil, then scoring along the lines with a metal straightedge and a sharp nail. Use acrylic or enamel paint to create a traditional Russian floral border similar to the one shown on the previous page, and paint the center in a checkerboard fashion. When the board is completely dry, apply several coats of spray varnish to protect it.

Sketch some designs for the chess pieces. You may wish to replace the king and queen with a czar and czarina, and the pawns with peasants. The rook could be radish-domed like St. Basil's Cathedral. Using clay or salt clay, form the pieces you have designed. Make the bases large enough so that the pieces do not tip. When pieces are completely dry (or fired), paint each set a different solid color, then use dabs of other bright colors to add details. Make the opposing sets easily distinguishable from each other.

Learn how to play the game with a friend.

Cathedral   Patriarch   Czar   Czarina   Cossack   Peasants

Russian Cooking

Russia is famous for exporting vodka and caviar and Russians enjoy both of these gourmet items, but tea, called *chai*, is the national drink served in large family urns, called *samovar*. Caviar served with cheese on bread is a popular appetizer.

Russian food varies, as might be expected by the country's vast size and differences in availability of foods. Cabbage and potatoes are staples of most European Russian diets, and beets are the basis for the famous Russian soup called *borscht*. In Siberia horse and reindeer meat are eaten and closer to China, oriental seasonings are common.

Russians who lived in frozen regions could be said to be the inventors of frozen food. An account written by two amazed English travelers in the eighteenth century revealed piles of cows, sheep, hogs, fowls, butter, eggs, and fish that were all stiffened into granite, and all for sale to be thawed and eaten. This concept was unknown to the English at that time. Many Russian foods are accompanied by sour cream. Beef Stroganov, created in the nineteenth century for Count Stroganov, a Russian diplomat, uses sour cream to create its rich sauce.

Activities and Projects

Try the Count's dish—Beef Stroganov.

> 2 lbs. lean beef, cut in 1/4" strips
> 1/4 c. vegetable oil
> 2 c. onions, thinly sliced
> 1 lb. fresh mushrooms, sliced
> 1 T. powdered mustard
> 1 T. sugar
> 1 t. salt
> 1 t. pepper
> 1 pint sour cream

Heat oil in a large skillet, and add the beef, half at a time, frying quickly for two to three minutes. Using a slotted spoon, remove beef onto a plate and add the mushrooms and onions to the skillet. Cover and simmer for 1/2 hour. Meanwhile, mix the mustard, sugar, and salt with a little water to form a paste. When onions are tender, add the meat, mustard mixture, sour cream, and pepper and heat. Taste for seasoning and add a little more salt or sugar to suit. Serve immediately, garnishing with shoestring potatoes.

To cool yourself down after the hot Stroganov, you may like to try this pureed fruit dessert that people in Russia enjoy during the hot summer months—Kisel.

Apple Kisel
2 lbs. apples, cut up
3 c. cold water
1/2 c. sugar
1 T. each cornstarch and water

Apricot Kisel
1 1/2 c. dried apricots
4 1/2 c. water
4 T. sugar
1 T. each cornstarch and water

Strawberry Kisel
2 1/2 pts. strawberries
2 c. cold water
3/4 c. sugar
1 T. each cornstarch and water

Cranberry Kisel
3 c. cranberries
2 c. cold water
3/4 c. sugar
1 T. each cornstarch and water

Boil the fruit in the water for about 15 minutes or until tender. Force the fruit through a fine sieve with the back of a spoon. Return the mixture to the pan. Combine the sugar and the starch and add to the mixture. Cook two to three minutes until the kisel begins to thicken. Cool to room temperature, then pour into dessert cups and refrigerate.

Bibliography

Constable, George, ed. *Library of Nations—The Soviet Union*. New York: Time-Life Books, Inc., 1984.

Florinsky, Michael T. *Encyclopedia of Russia and the Soviet Union*. New York: McGraw Hill, 1961.

Lye, Keith. *Take a Trip to Russia*. London: Franklin Watts, Ltd., 1982.

Recipes From Foods of the World. Time-Life Books.

Resnick, Abraham. *Commonwealth of Independent States*. Chicago: Childrens Press, Inc., 1993.

Schuman, Jo Miles. *Art From Many Hands*. Worchester, MA: Davis Publications, Inc., 1981.

Thayer, Charles W. *Russia—Life World Library*. New York: Time, Inc., 1962.

Wallace, Robert. *Rise of Russia*. New York: Time, Inc., 1967.

Cimmerian Pottery
1000 – 700 B.C.

AUSTRALIA

The continent of Australia is a work of art like none other on earth. Australia separated from other land masses so long ago that it evolved its own unique forms of plants and animals (such as the pouched marsupials). It was uninhabited by man until the aborigines came some 40,000 years ago, probably from the Javanese islands to the north. They developed a simple way of life in this harsh land and produced art forms that echoed their beliefs and reverence for the earth. The rest of the world had believed that land existed to the south since A.D. 150 when Ptolemy reasoned the lands in the north must be balanced by something. The name *Australia* comes from the Latin, *australis* which means "southern." It was not until the 1600s and 1700s that the Dutch and the British explored and settled Australia. Since World War II, immigrants from 100 different countries have made Australia their home.

The art and culture (and even the language) of this "Land Down Under" is an interesting blend, as all these various peoples have come together and influenced one another.

83

Aboriginal Rock Painting

Deep in the red center of Australia, so called because of the red color of the iron oxide in the sands, lies Uluru, or Ayers Rock, a huge red stone mountain jutting 1,142 feet into the sky. Though this rock is a popular climbing attraction for tourists (the aborigines call them *minga rama*, or "climbing ants"), it has been considered sacred for centuries among the aborigines who still perform ceremonies there. The gigantic rock is filled with caves that have been painted with sacred figures from "Dreamtime." According to the aborigines, the First People, supernatural beings, roamed the earth before any other people and gave it form. One such spirit is the Namarrgon, or Lightning Man, whose head and elbows are clad with stone axes to split the clouds and trees. Today, each tree and rock contains the spirit of an ancestor so the bond with nature is very strong. At Uluru and throughout Australia, aboriginal artists recorded not only depictions of "Dreamtime," but also successful hunts, animals of Australia, and even the British sailing ships spotted on the seas. They used finely ground clay rich in iron ore, ochre, and charcoal to create rusty red, golden yellow, black, and white. The powder is mixed with water and liquid from an orchid as a fixative and applied with feathers, fingers, or twigs frayed at the ends.

Activities and Projects

Try your hand at rock painting. Select a large flat rock and create an "aboriginal" design in the style of those illustrated on the following page to fit the shape of your rock. Prepare your paints as the aborigines did by crushing and grinding various earth tone pigments between rounded stones or with a mortar and pestle. Try charcoal, clay (some areas of the United States have red or golden earth), rust, chalk, and conte crayons, or use your imagination as the aborigines did to invent new sources of color. When pigments are ground to powder, add water to make a thin paste. Collect twigs and feathers to serve as brushes and use these creative brushes to finish your painting. Today, for convenience, the aboriginal artists take advantage of modern technology and substitute brushes and paint bowls when available. You may wish to do the same!

ULURU

Totems and Bark Painting

The aboriginal people of Australia are said to be simple and primitive. It is true that as a nomadic people they did not create huge temples or homes, and because of the hot climate, they wore no clothes. They carried no weapons except for spears and boomerangs, so they had very few material possessions. But the culture of the aborigines was not simple at all. They felt they were one with nature and developed their beliefs and religion, called "totemism," based on careful observation of natural phenomena. Each group within a tribe had a sacred animal, or totem, possessing powers and skills which it passed on to the group. Aborigines painted themselves with symbols of their totem animal and mimicked that animal's actions in ceremonial dances. The totems also appear on rock paintings and on bark paintings. To prepare a piece of eucalyptus bark for painting, aboriginal artists singe and scrape it, then flatten it under stones. They use the same pigments and application techniques as they use for stone paintings. Though artists today have more permanent oil paints, many prefer to use ancient techniques. The "X-ray" style used to paint some of these totem animals is most unusual. The outline of the animal is filled in with the backbones, muscles, and inner organs of the animal. Other bark paintings may depict episodes from the clan's history, or "Dreamtime," or a successful hunt.

Today the art of bark painting is greatly valued by all Australians and also tourists. Aborigines are encouraged to make and sell their work. Some of the pieces command high prices and not only supplements their income, but ensures that this ancient art form remains alive.

Activities and Projects

Create your own aboriginal bark painting. Study the "X-ray" style and other bark painting examples shown here, then sketch your own design of your totem animal. You may wish to familiarize yourself with your animal's internal structure so that you can paint it "X-ray" style with some accuracy. Use a thin rough piece of wood or heavy cardboard as bark and the same paints as described for rock painting, or use regular tempera paints in rich earth tones.

FS-10146 Crafts From Other Cultures

An Ancient Aboriginal Lifestyle ————————————

The aborigines were hunter-gatherers. They did not plant crops or raise herds of animals; they roamed from place to place constructing quick shelters to last only until food supplies ran low and then moved on. They may have been the first environmentalists. They knew that if they gathered all the plant food in an area or killed all the animals, there would be no new growth when they returned, so they always left a little of everything so the fragile environment was not altered. The men carried their weapons at all times and did the hunting of larger game. The women gathered edible roots, plants, and berries, and even the children searched for small animals, grubs, and insects that were good to eat. Though aborigines were continually on the move, they did stay within a certain range. This was because they could survive more easily where they knew the food and water sources, and because they were careful to respect the territories of other tribes nearby. When it was time to move on, the women packed their few belongings into baskets they wove from long grasses or bark fibers and decorated with traditional designs.

Activities and Projects ————————————

Weave an aboriginal basket in which to carry your possessions. Begin by studying the one shown on the following page and determine how yours will look. Sketch some motifs such as those found in aboriginal art. Cut a circle 8" in diameter from heavy cardboard or mat board and use a compass to divide the edge into 60 roughly equal parts. Cut 1/4" deep notches at each of the 60 divisions. Cut 30 strands of raffia or jute 5' each and fold in half. Placing the halfway mark in the center of the cardboard circle, press the strands into the notches across the diameter. Repeat the process until all strands have been placed and tie a loose knot in the back to keep the excess out of your way for the time being. Begin weaving by tucking another strand measuring about 6' under one of the threaded strands near the center of the cardboard and pulling it through halfway. Give the strand a half twist and thread it around the next strand. Repeat this process around and around the center of the cardboard, working out as you go. When the weaving strand runs short, tie on additional strands, tucking the knots to the inside each time. When you get near the edge of the cardboard, you will have finished the base of the basket. Remove the cardboard carefully, untie the loose knot, and continue to weave, keeping your circles the same size to form the sides. To make the weaving easier, punch two holes in the bottom of an oatmeal box, place it inside the weaving, and thread a string through the holes, through the base of the weaving, and tie them to a doorknob as you continue to weave. As you finish your basket, begin to make the circles a little larger to form the top edge. Finally, trim the strands to about 2", fold them over along the upper lip of the basket and secure them by weaving the final circle over and over to form a coil effect as shown. Stuff your basket with newspaper to hold it firm, and paint it with your design using temperas, acrylics, or aboriginal paints in rich earth tones. Attach a braid of rafia 2' long at opposite sides of the top for a handle.

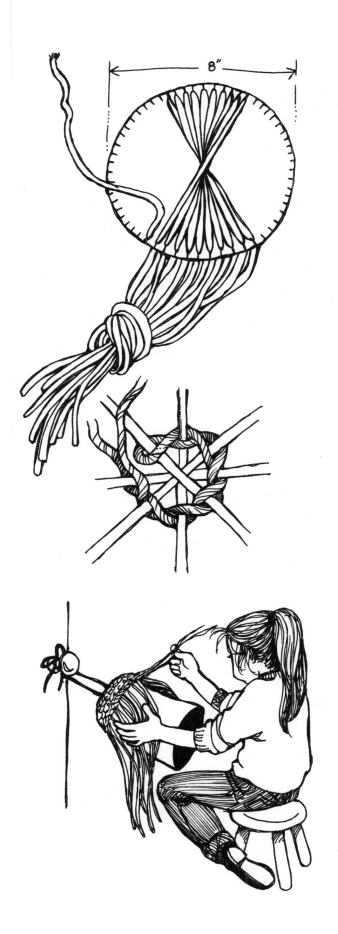

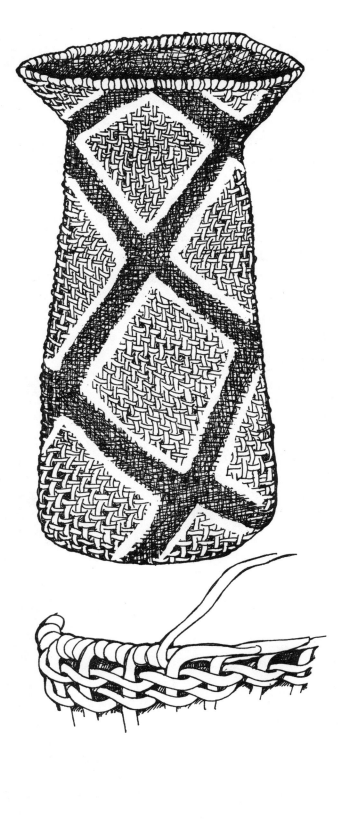

Boomerangs, Corroborees, and Didjeridus

The aborigines hold secret ceremonies to initiate young males into adulthood. Females are not allowed to attend and are warned away by the "bull-roarer," a slat of wood tied to the end of a hair string that makes a roaring noise when twirled.

Everyone is invited to attend a *corroboree*, an evening of singing and dancing held to relate important news in the form of dance, to retell ancient legends of ancestors, and to have a good time. The corroboree grounds are prepared by the elders of the tribe. They lay down white dust in elaborate patterns significant to the story which will be related in the dance. Most corroborees have a series of concentric circles worked into the design somewhere with a diameter of 12' or more.

Music is provided by clapsticks and *didjeridus*, which are hollow trees or bamboo, sometimes plain, sometimes elaborately decorated, about 4" in diameter and 3' to 7' long. They are blown through one end, producing a loud, dull sound.

Aboriginal warriors paint themselves with designs dictated by their totems and dance the stories of a successful hunt, waving their traditional weapons—spears, spear-throwers (*woomara*), and boomerangs. There are two types of boomerangs—the non-returning variety (heavy, less curved and used for hunting) and the returning type (lighter, smaller and used mostly for fun and show).

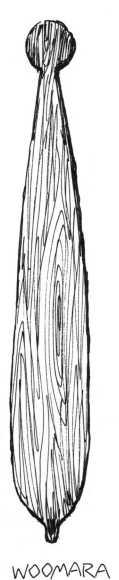

BOOMERANGS

WOOMARA
(spear thrower)

DIDJERIDU

Activities and Projects ————————

Make your own didjeridu. You may be adventurous enough to try to hollow out a small tree or remove the inner chambers of a piece of bamboo, but perhaps it would be easier to start with a long cardboard tube like those used to mail posters or a piece of 3" or 4" plastic pipe. Decorate it by painting it a wood tone (rough up plastic pipe with sandpaper so the paint will adhere), and then add traditional aboriginal designs.

Decorate two sticks with aboriginal designs for clapsticks. Carve a returning type of boomerang from a lightweight wood such as balsa. One end should be twisted slightly upwards and the other end downwards as it is this contra-twist that gives the boomerang its unique returning action. Decorate it with traditional designs.

Through English Eyes

When explorers from Europe first arrived in Australia, they were astounded with the strange plants and animals that inhabited this new land. When tales of creatures such as the kangaroo, wombat, lola, platypus, and spiny anteater were first reported "back home," people laughed in disbelief. Captain James Cook was one such explorer who set sail from Plymouth, England, in 1768. Sailing with him was Joseph Banks, a wealthy young botanist from London who is known as "the father of Australia" because he convinced the British government to establish a colony there. Also on board were two naturalists and two artists who took advantage of the times the ship docked for repairs to collect many specimens of the plant life and to make many detailed drawings of what they discovered there.

Activities and Projects

Imagine you are a naturalist studying the unusual flora and fauna of Australia. You have been assigned to produce accurate drawings for people who have never been there. Look through magazines or books to find a good photograph of a plant or animal found nowhere else but Australia. You may be able to observe an actual specimen if you live near a zoo or a botanical garden. Make a preliminary sketch of your species on tracing paper or other lightweight paper, then using a lightboard or window, transfer the sketch onto a heavy weight paper such as watercolor paper. Carefully outline with a fine line of India ink or permanent marker, allow to dry completely, then color in the drawing as accurately as possible with watercolor washes. In your best old-fashioned script handwriting, copy the scientific name of your species, and the common name in small block letters underneath it.

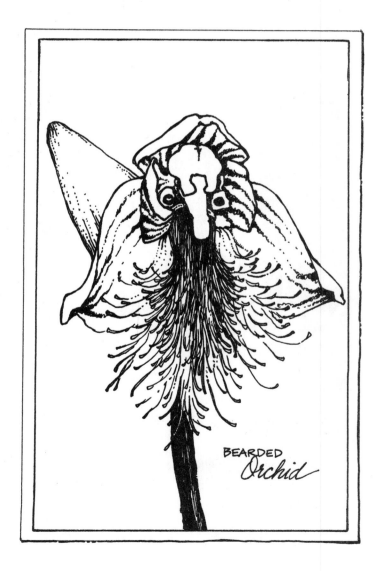

BEARDED Orchid

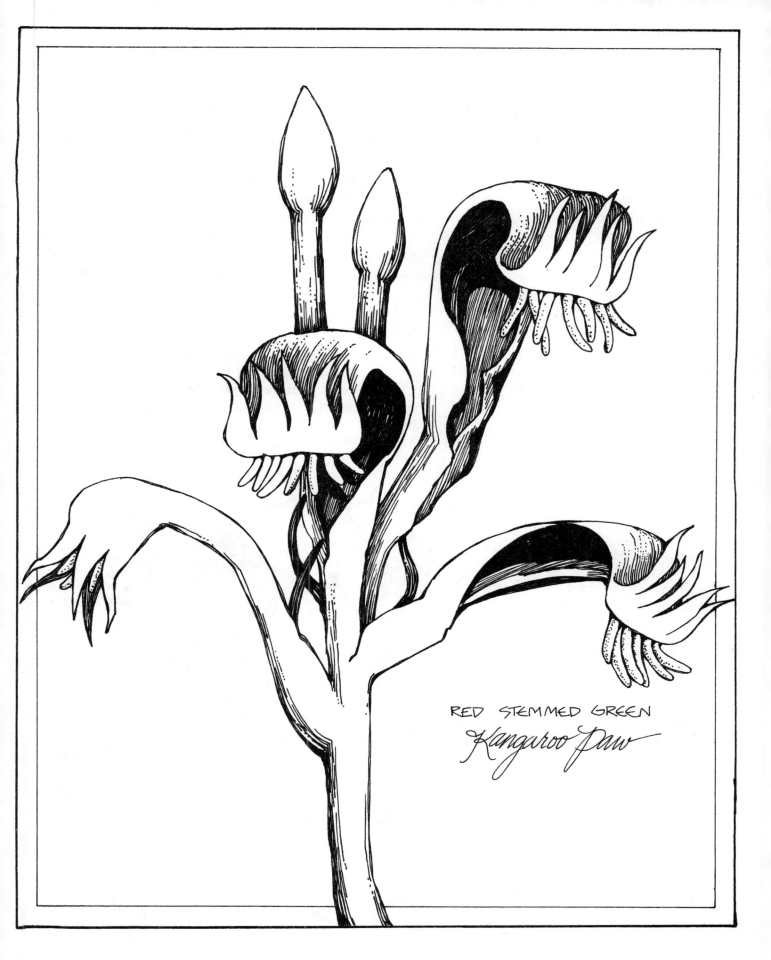

RED STEMMED GREEN
Kangaroo Paw

FS-10146 Crafts From Other Cultures

Authentic Australian

The first language spoken in Australia was, of course, the language of the aborigines. Since they were isolated from the rest of the world, the aborigines developed a language totally unrelated to any other. Though there were over 500 tribes with different dialects all over Australia, most were able to communicate through sign language, common phrases, and similarities in speech.

Today, the vast majority of Australians, 99 percent in fact, speak English, but the "Aussies" have added their own touches to give the language a definite Australian twist. Below are some examples.

avago: try it
barney: argument
barrack: to jeer or cheer your team
battler: someone who never gives up
big smoke: outback term for the city
billy: tin can for boiling water
bush: any wooded area, back country
bush tucker: wild eats
crook: broken or sick
drongo: fool
fair dinkum: honest
fair go: even chance
garbo: garbage man
gibber plains: stony wetlands
good on you: good for you
greenie: environmental activist
grouse: excellent
hard yacker: tough work
hoon: idiot
humpy: small hut
jack-up: reject
jumbuck: sheep
larrikin: a young rascal
mate: pal
mob: group of people, sheep, cattle
no worries: no problems
outback: back country
picnic: a big mess
pommy: Britisher, not complimentary
ratbag: strange person
ropeable: furious
she'll be right: it will be okay
shivoo: party
skite: to boast

squib: coward
sticky-beak: a nosy person
tucker: meal
up a gum tree: in trouble
whinge: complain
willy-willy: windstorm
wowser: stick in the mud

Activities and Projects

Australians are an easygoing, laid-back people with a great sense of humor. Some say their comraderie developed because the life was so hard that everyone had to work together. Use the examples given and your knowledge of Australia to create a "Land Down Under" comic strip. Feature Australian wildlife such as kangaroos, wallabies, wombats, and platypi. Let the action take place with an Aussie backdrop–Uluru, Sydney Harbour, or the Great Barrier Reef. So get out your pencil and paper and "Give it a burl, cobber." (Try it, pal.)

Great Barrier Reef

The Great Barrier Reef runs for 1,200 miles off the coast of Queensland, in northeast Australia. Nowhere else in the world is there so much coral in one place. This massive collection of islands has taken 15,000 years to accumulate from the limestone casings of polyps; it measures 120' high from the ocean floor and a mile wide in some places. The reef was responsible for many early shipwrecks. A Spanish captain, Luis Vaez de Torres, accidentally discovered the reef when he sailed from Peru and was blown off course in a monsoon. During a voyage in 1768, French explorer Bougainville took one look at the reef and turned right around! It caused Cook's vessel, the *Endeavor*, to spring a leak in 1770, but he managed to make it safely to shore and make repairs.

Today, the major dangers of the reef are the sharks, stonefish, barracuda, giant clams, and 400 different varieties of razor-sharp coral. Skin divers, scuba divers, and photographers face all of these as they explore this underwater paradise. Mud from Daintree River has suffocated the life out of a portion of the reef near the river's mouth, but in 1975 the Great Barrier Reef Marine Park was established to see that it is protected from further pollution.

Activities and Projects

Build your own miniature Great Barrier Reef. Study the lifeforms that coexist in the delicate ecosystem such as brain coral, staghorn coral, mushroom coral, rosy coral, sea anenomes, jellyfish, pearl oysters, green turtles, starfish, shellfish, whale sharks, nurse sharks, devil rays, stonefish, barracuda, giant clams, stripeys, blennies, banner fish, blue and green demoiselles, orange spotted leatherjackets, beaked coralfish, clownfish, butterfly cod, filefish, gurnards, toados, ribbon fish, eels, baromater crabs, and bluebottle fish.

Lay a sturdy cardboard box on its side as if you are creating a stage. Cut a piece of posterboard or stiff paper the inside height of your box and long enough so that it will fit from one side of the box, around the back on the inside to the opposite side. Use tempera or acrylics to paint a faint background of reefs and schools of fish on the posterboard and place it inside the box for a background. Form the reef from rocks and build it up with salt clay, cooked clay, or modeling clay, forming the various species of coral you have researched. Pinch form each fish and use a needle to poke a thread through it before the clay hardens to suspend the fish from the ceiling. Some fish may be glued to the reef as if they are swimming very near. When all your creations have dried, choose the brightest, most exotic colors to paint these wonderful species and put them all in their places.

Decorate the outside of the box with a scene of the Great Barrier Reef from a distance and attach letters to form a title "Australia's Great Barrier Reef" across the box. You may also wish to attach a list of the specimens you include and their locations on your mini-reef.

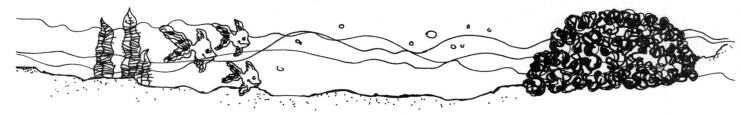

Australia's Great Barrier Reef

Sydney Opera House

If Uluru Rock and the Great Barrier Reef are the most recognized of Australia's natural wonders, then the Sydney Opera House is the best known man-made wonder. This symbol of modern Australia was built in 1973 on the harbour near where, just two centuries earlier, the first settlers landed as prisoners sentenced to Australia's Botany Bay penal colony. The Opera House was designed by a Dane, Joern Utzon, whose design was selected from over 200 international entries. Its roof rises 216' at its highest peak and resembles the sails that are often seen in Sydney Harbour, such as the fleet of windsurfers which sets off from Manly Beach during the Festival of Sydney. Sailboat and yacht races often take place in the harbour, also.

Activities and Projects

Using the wind in sails for your inspiration, design and construct a replica of Sydney's famous Opera House. Study the drawings shown and copy the pattern according to the size you want onto some stiff white paper such as posterboard, watercolor paper, or oaktag. Using a hot glue gun or white glue, and tape carefully assemble the pieces onto a stiff piece of cardboard, foam-core, masonite, or a paneling scrap that has been painted a deep blue to resemble water. As a finishing touch, add some colorful sails around the structure and a bright label.

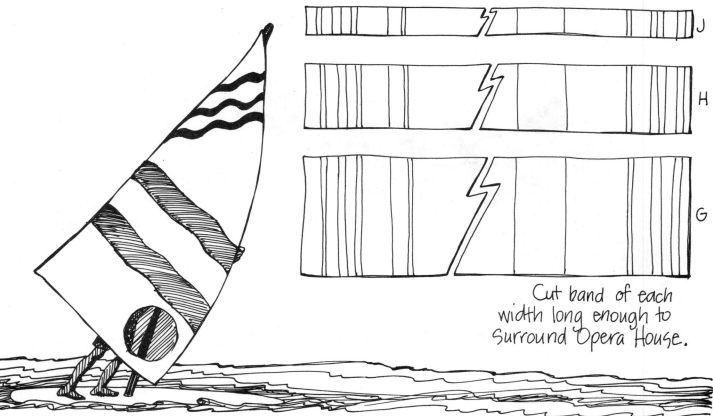

J

H

G

Cut band of each width long enough to surround Opera House.

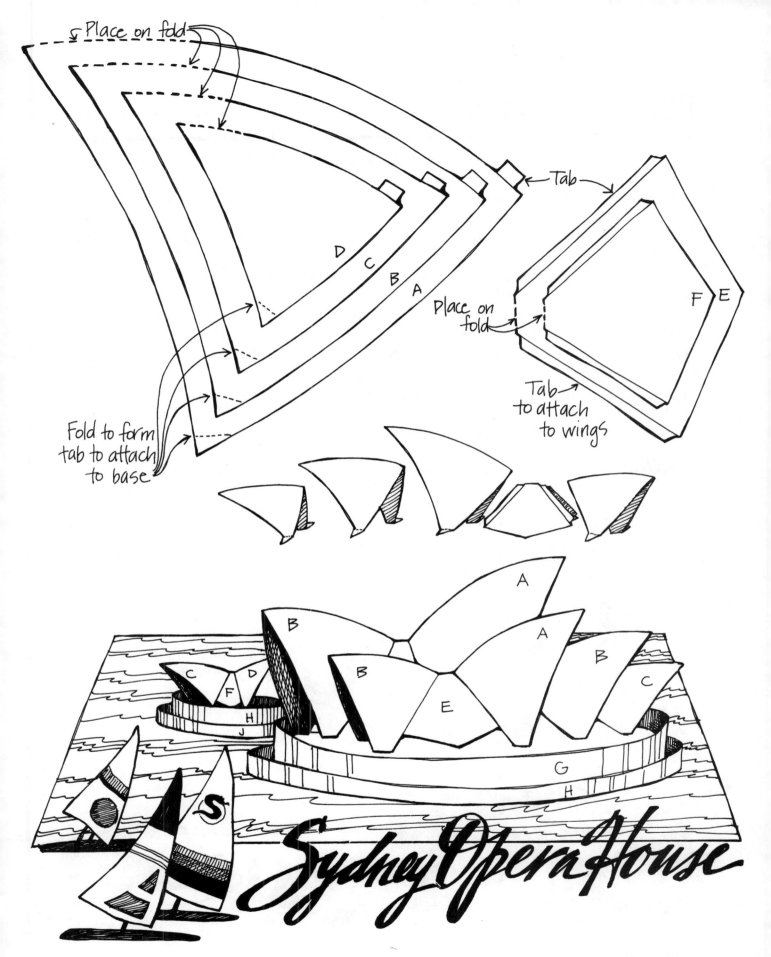

Place on fold

Tab

Place on fold

Fold to form tab to attach to base

Tab to attach to wings

D C B A

F E

A

B

A

C B

B

D

F

E

H

J

G

H

Sydney Opera House

FS-10146 Crafts From Other Cultures

Dinner Down Under

Since the bulk of the population of Australia is of British origin, it is not surprising that the cuisine of Australia is similar to that of Britain. A typical meal for an Australian family would be roasted meat, potato, and vegetable. Meat pies are popular snacks, and perhaps because of so much sunny weather, barbecues are popular. Immigrants from Italy, Greece, Hungary, and, more recently, Asian countries have all added their own flavors and spices to Australian cooking.

Like any group of people anywhere, the aborigines ate what was available to them from the land, but their diet seems very unusual to us today. Kangaroos, emus, and goanna lizards were among their usual fare, as were insects, birds' eggs, and snails. They pounded seeds to make a cake-like bread and satisfied the sweet tooth with honey from bees and honey ants. The wichety grub, larvae stage of a moth species, was roasted and relished.

A more common and tamer Australian food is called *damper bread*, probably named after the English buccaneer William Dampier who visited the northeast and northwest coasts of Australia in 1688 and 1699. Since colonial times, it has been a traditional part of the diet of the outback workers and was baked in a camp oven buried in embers.

Activities and Projects

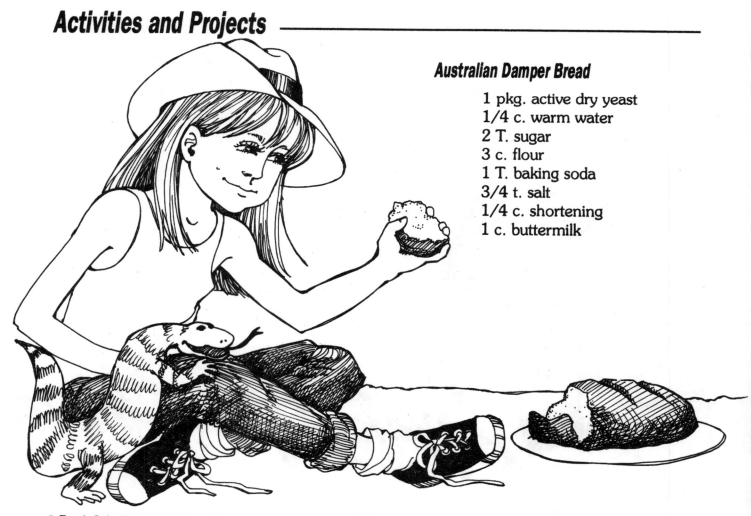

Australian Damper Bread

1 pkg. active dry yeast
1/4 c. warm water
2 T. sugar
3 c. flour
1 T. baking soda
3/4 t. salt
1/4 c. shortening
1 c. buttermilk

Stir the yeast into warm water and add sugar. Mix flour, salt, and baking powder together in a large bowl and work in shortening with your clean fingers until the mixture is crumbly. Add yeast mixture and buttermilk and blend until soft dough forms. Knead dough on floured surface about 1 minute, then let rest 10 minutes. Form into a ball on a greased cookie sheet, cover, and let rise for 30 minutes. Cut an X 1/2" deep across the top of the loaf and bake in a 375° oven for 35 minutes. Tear bread to pieces while it is still warm and enjoy it with butter, jam, or a wichety grub or two!

Australian Caramel Bananas

Satisfy your sweet tooth with this Australian favorite.

Heat 2/3 c. brown sugar, 2 T. whipping cream, and 1 T. butter over low heat, gently stirring until sugar is dissolved. Stir in 1 t. rum flavoring and cool in the refrigerator for an hour. Slice 4 bananas crosswise and lengthwise and arrange in 4 serving bowls. Top with caramel sauce, garnish with whipped cream, and sprinkle with toasted almonds.

Bibliography

Baker, Eleanor. *The Australian Aborigines*. Austin: Steck Vaugn Company, 1968.

Baker, Eleanor. *Australia Today*. Austin: Steck Vaugn Company, 1969.

Constable, George, editor. *Australia–Library of Nations*. Amsterdam: Time-Life Books, Inc., 1985.

Crocker, Betty, pseud. *Betty Crocker's International Cookbook*. New York: Random House, 1980.

Crocker, Betty, pseud. *Betty Crocker's International Cookbook*. New York: Prentice Hall, 1989.

Harrell, Mary Ann. *Surprising Lands Down Under*. Washington, D.C.: National Geographic Society, 1989.

Holland, Julian. *Lands of the Southern Cross*. London: Aldus Books, Ltd., 1971.

Lepthien, Emilie U. *Australia–Enchantment of the World*. Chicago: Childrens Press, 1982.

MacInnes, Colin. *Australia and New Zealand*. New York: Time Inc., 1964.

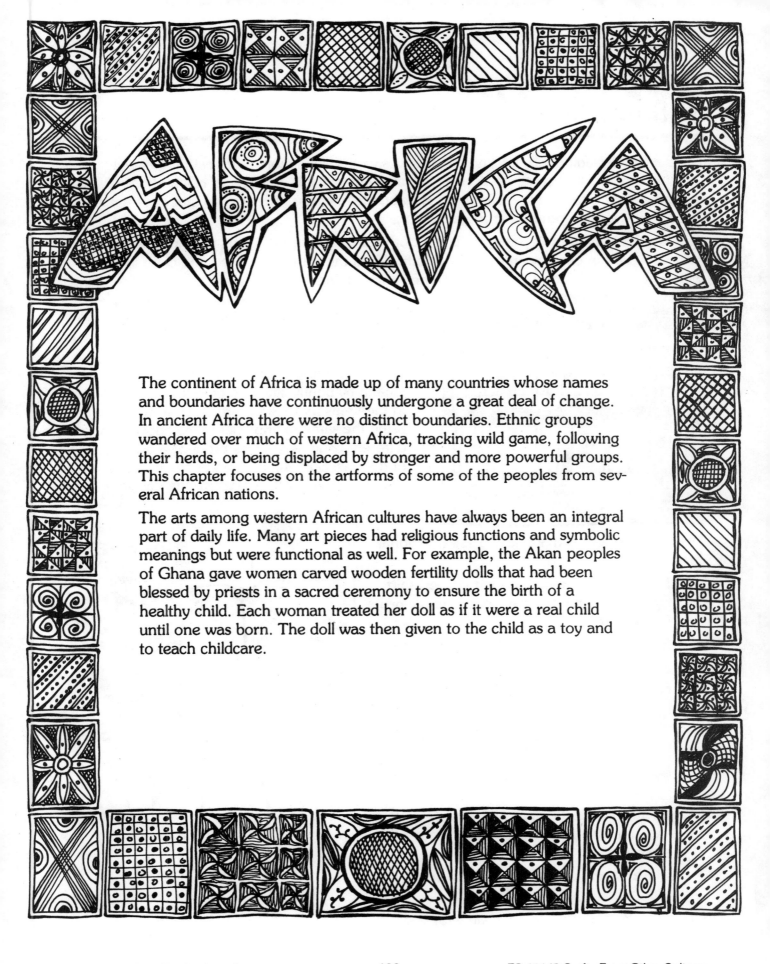

AFRICA

The continent of Africa is made up of many countries whose names and boundaries have continuously undergone a great deal of change. In ancient Africa there were no distinct boundaries. Ethnic groups wandered over much of western Africa, tracking wild game, following their herds, or being displaced by stronger and more powerful groups. This chapter focuses on the artforms of some of the peoples from several African nations.

The arts among western African cultures have always been an integral part of daily life. Many art pieces had religious functions and symbolic meanings but were functional as well. For example, the Akan peoples of Ghana gave women carved wooden fertility dolls that had been blessed by priests in a sacred ceremony to ensure the birth of a healthy child. Each woman treated her doll as if it were a real child until one was born. The doll was then given to the child as a toy and to teach childcare.

The Fabric of Africa

Africans have traditionally adorned themselves with scarification, body painting, jewelry, and clothing made from beautifully decorated cloth. For festivals and special celebrations, Asantis in Ghana may wear Kente cloth which is elaborately woven with designs that have been handed down from generation to generation.

The Yoruba people of Nigeria produce a cloth called "Adire Eleko" by painting a cassava starch mixture in designs onto a white cloth. When the starch has dried, the cloth is dyed with indigo (called "adire"), a dye from the chopped and pounded leaves of the indigo plant.

The starched areas resist the dye while background takes on brown color which immediately oxidizes with the air and becomes a beautiful deep blue color. "Adire Eleso" cloth, or "Tie-Dye" as we call it, is also produced in Nigeria, Togo, and Ghana by tightly stitching or tieing off the fabric in the areas that are to remain light, then dying it using the same method described above. Many different tying techniques produce a broad range of designs. Sometimes rows of small stones (called "eleso") are tied off to produce the design.

The finished cloth is made into these traditional garments:

Dashike—a loose-fitting, long-sleeved shirt worn with pants, or a long version worn as a gown.

Sokotos—baggy pants worn by men with a short dashike

Agbada—Yoruba dashike

Lapa—Yoruba woman's skirt made from a large piece of cloth wrapped around the body and tied at the waist.

Buba—Yoruba woman's scoop-necked blouse

Iborun—Yoruba woman's large sash worn with a lapa and buba and tied around the waist

Oja—an even larger sash to carry bundles or children

Gele—Yoruba woman's turban wrapped from a cloth measuring 1' x 6'

104   FS-10146 Crafts From Other Cultures

Activities and Projects

Create your own "Adire Eleko" cloth. Select white cotton fabric such as an old sheet or dish-towel. (Sometimes hospitals will give away worn sheets.) After studying the traditional designs shown here, plan your design on paper the size of your fabric in the same style. Make your resist concoction by whisking together 3/4 c. flour, 2 T. alum, and 4 c. cold water, cooking mixture over low heat until it thickens, then cooling it. The mixture should be about as thick as white glue. Pour the starch into a plastic squeeze bottle and draw your design onto your fabric by squeezing a bead of glue along the lines, or paint it directly onto the fabric with a small brush. When the fabric is completely dry, dip it into prepared commercial dye, following the instructions. Use any dark color desired, but indigo blue (bluejean blue) is most authentic. While the dyed, rinsed cloth is still damp and the resist is softened, scrape it off the fabric with a sharp knife or scraper. Dry and iron.

Now try "Adire Eleso." Using the same type of fabric, tie, stitch, and twist it to create the desired pattern. Use tiny orthodontic rubber bands to tie rows of small seeds or stones. Fold and stitch small tight pleats. Create concentric circles by pulling up the center and tying off the fabric at intervals down from the center. Or simply fold the fabric and dip the corners into the dye.

Adire Eleko

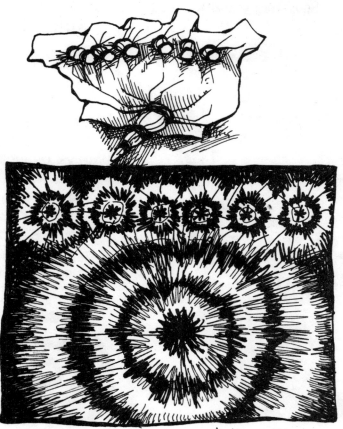

Adire Eleso

Funeral Fabric

Funerals in Ghana are not sad affairs; they are more like family reunions when relatives from all over the country come together in celebration of the end of life on earth and the beginning of the spirit life. Everyone shares the expenses of the singing, drumming, dancing, and feasting that occurs. Traditionally Ghanaians wear clothing made from rusty red and black "Adinkra" cloth (*adinkra* means "good-bye"). A black dye made from the bark of a tree is used to paint or print designs with stamps cut from dried calabash gourds onto the rusty-colored fabric. The designs used are beautifully decorative and also have symbolic meanings. Today "adinkra cloth" is made from long strips of white or bright-colored cloth and stitched together with embroidered stripes of red, yellow, green, and black.

Activities and Projects

Make an "Adinkra" wall hanging. Study the symbols and designs shown, then plan your own design. You may want to combine the two techniques of painting with a small brush (traditionally sticks are used) and printing with symbol stamps. Cut the stamps from potatoes, Styrofoam meat trays, or linoleum blocks if there are no calabashes handy. Make certain each stamp will fit into a 3" x 3" space. Cut and iron strips of cotton sheeting about 13" wide. Beginning about 1/2" from the edges, divide your fabric into rectangles about 18" long. Use a small paintbrush or plastic comb dipped into acrylic paint that has been thinned to the consistency of heavy cream.

Further divide your cloth as your design dictates and paint in the line designs with the brush. Use a brush to cover the bottom of the stamps with the same acrylic, and carefully press the painted stamp onto your cloth. Keep a scrap to use for trial runs before painting anything. When paint is completely dry, press the cloth once more, turning the edges under about 1/4". Use red, yellow, green, and black embroidery floss to join the strips together as shown.

Chokwe Basketry

The Chokwe people of Angola and Zaire are not only masters at carving in wood, but they also create beautiful designs in basketry for decorative purposes and everyday use. These baskets, called *kambalas*, are woven into patterns out of reeds from the river.

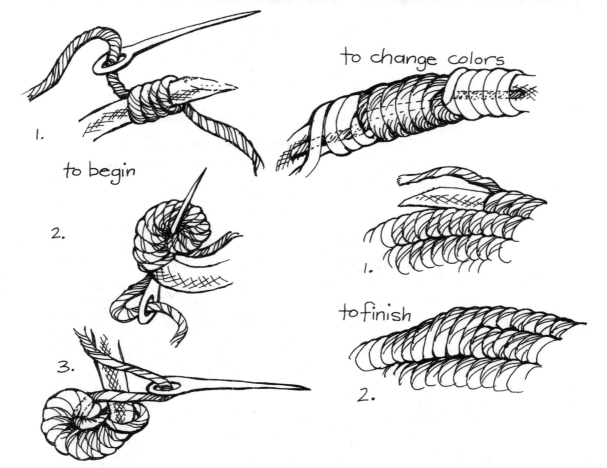

to change colors

to begin

1.

2.

3.

1.

to finish

2.

Activities and Projects

Make a Chokwe basket. Study the traditional designs shown. Then sketch a design of your own in the Chokwe style. The Chokwe use natural dyes of rusts and chocolate brown to tint the straw-colored reeds, so work these and other earthtones into your design. You will need some clothesline or any other similar pliable rope for the core of your weaving and also yarn, rafia, any long natural fibers, or actual reeds that have been dried. If you use reeds, once they have dried to their natural tannish color, they can be tinted with fabric dyes. As you weave the basket, keep reeds soaking in a pan until you need them. Begin trimming about 1/2" of the end of the rope at an angle. Wrap the string around the rope for about 1", leaving a short tail of string free. Work the wrapped rope around to form a tight circle and use the tail of string to help secure it. This is the trickiest part. Continue wrapping the string around the rope, making a figure 8 with the string at intervals of 1/2" to 3/4" to fasten the wrapped rope to the growing center circle. When your string runs out, or it is time to add another color as your design dictates, lay the end of the new color along the rope and wrap around it a few times to hold it, then lay the original color along the rope and wrap it with the new color. When you have added as much of the new color as you need, cut if off with 1" excess, and continue to wrap with the original color. If you need to add more rope core, cut the old and new rope ends at angles and apply a dot of white glue where they meet. You do not need to wait until the glue dries. If your piece is to be bowl-shaped, gradually raise the rope as you wrap. When the design is complete, wrap a final circle of the last color and trim the rope at an angle again and wrap around it and the previous row at the same time until all the rope has been covered.

Golden Ornaments

Among many west African peoples it is easy to tell a person's status by the clothes he or she wears, scarification, hairstyles, or other special objects such as hats, beads, amulets, staffs, and golden objects.

In Ghana, the chiefs of the Akan people have control of the gold, and they wear it in the form of beautiful medallions around their necks to display their high status.

Young male officials of the Asantes wear *Akrafokonmu*, or "soul-washer's disks," because they are responsible for keeping the Asantehene's (king's) soul clean by performing rites of purification. These disks are hung around the neck on a long cord made of twisted white pineapple fibers. Besides the soul-washers, kings, chiefs and swordbearers also wear these neckpieces on ceremonial occasions.

The medallions are made of gold through several different processes. Sometimes they are hammered from a sheet of gold, and at other times they are caste from melted gold poured into a mold.

Activities and Projects

Make a soul-washer's disk. Study the designs shown here and then sketch a design of your own in the traditional west African style. Using a wooden dowel sharpened to a blunt point, trace your design onto 36–38 gauge tooling foil in gold or brass cut slightly larger than the finished medallion (available in art supply stores or from catalogues). Place a thick layer of newspaper under your foil as you complete your medallion, pressing from the front or the back as your design dictates. Cut around the edges you have traced, leaving 1/8" to 1/4" extra around the piece, and carefully fold that portion back to finish the edges. On a

bound medallion, you may have to use scissors to make tiny clips each 1/4" to 1/2" before you fold under the edges of the circular medallions. Punch a small hole on each side and attach white string (or pineapple fibers) so that your medallion will hang around your neck to the middle of your chest.

Just as the Africans used various methods in fashioning these pieces, you may want to try alternative methods of making "faux" golden medallions.

Use oil clay to form a mold, scraping out the areas you want to be raised. Fill the mold with plaster of paris prepared as the instructions indicate. When the plaster has hardened, carefully remove the clay, clean and dry the plaster thoroughly, and give it one or two coats of gold spray paint.

Cut out your medallion shape from heavy cardboard or mat board. Twist worm-shaped rolls of tissue paper and use hot glue or white glue to attach them to your medallion along the lines you have designed. You may need to use strategically placed straight pins to hold the twists in place until the glue sets. When the medallion's design is finished and completely dry, spray both sides with gold spray paint.

 FS-10146 Crafts From Other Cultures

Masks, Masks, and More Masks

Masks appear as integral parts of life in almost every west African culture. According to the Wee peoples of the Ivory Coast and Liberia, masks are often frightful symbols of wild spirits that reinforce the importance of following society's rules. They are thought to scare away the evils that disrupt orderly life. The Bamana of Mali have a mask representing each of the six instructional stages through which a youth must pass toward adulthood. Some masks, such as the "Zo ge" mask of the Dan peoples in Liberia, are thought to help cure diseases whose causes are unknown. The Ijo made masks to represent the "owu" or water spirits who ensured fertility and food supply. The masks were worn to honor these spirits in special ceremonies. Often white was used on masks used in funeral celebrations since it was considered a symbol of peace and the afterlife by the Punu people of Gabon. The Senufos from Mali and the Ivory Coast initiated their dead into the afterlife so the deceased, male or female, would help the living of the village to handle the spirits.

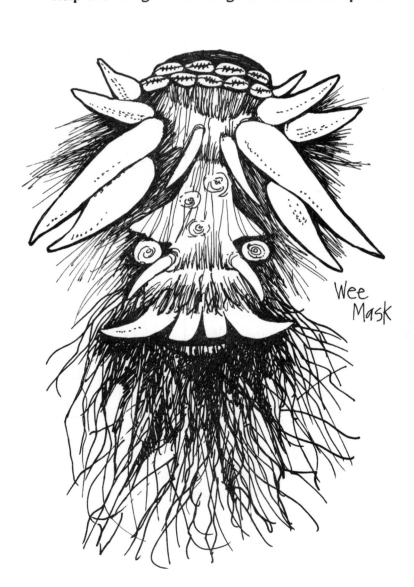

Wee Mask

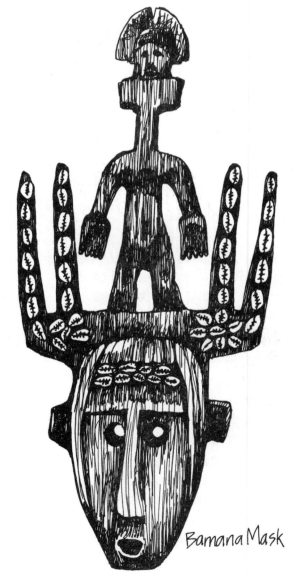

Bamana Mask

Dan Mask

Punu Mask

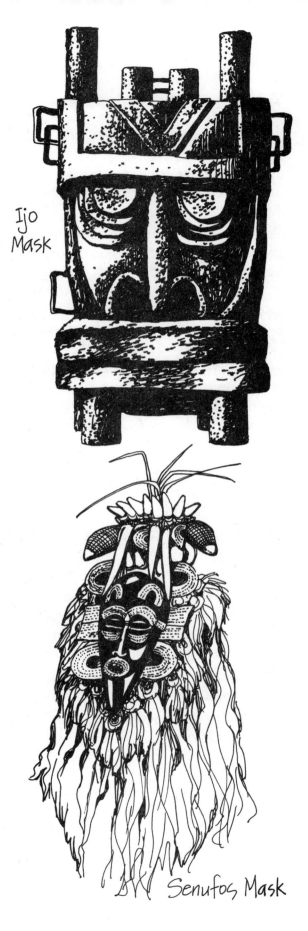

Ijo Mask

Senufos Mask

113

Activities and Projects

Masks have always been made of just about anything that is available–cowrie shells, fiber, hair, cloth, teeth, horn, wood, copper and other metals, feathers, seeds, ceramic, and various pigments. Some of their abstract forms seem to have influenced some of the great modern artists such as Pablo Picasso. Allow their forms to influence you as you create your own African mask masterpiece!

Begin your project by studying the examples of African masks such as those shown on the previous pages, then designing one of your own in a traditional style. Scavenge around for objects to add to your mask that will make it interesting just as Africans do. With assorted materials assembled, construct the base of your mask. If you have access to woodworking tools, you may want to try your hand at carving a mask from wood you have picked up in the forest. Use a saw or ax to form the general shape and finer woodcarving set for the details. Hammer nails and brass brads for details. Paint it with rich earth tones and apply brown shoe polish, then burnish it so that it appears old.

Papier mache is a good material to use for a mask. Blow up a face-sized balloon and build up layers of newspaper strips that have been dipped in a mixture of thin wallpaper paste over the balloon. Use wadded newspaper, cardboard, egg cartons, paper rolls, pressed cardboard drink holders, and most of all your ingenuity to create interesting additions to your mask. Tape all of these in place with pasted strips. It is sometimes helpful to allow the piece to dry overnight so it is stiffer and stronger. Apply a final layer of paper towel strips over the entire mask, allow it to dry thoroughly, then paint with tempera or acrylic paint. Glue on feathers, shells, metal, rafia, or yarn to finish the mask.

Use terra cotta clay, cooked clay, or salt clay for a mask. Begin with a slab of clay rolled out to 1/2" thickness draped over a head-sized wad of newspaper. Cut out holes for eyes and build up protuberances (noses, lips, horns, ears) by pinching and adding pieces of clay. Press beads and shells into the soft clay for details. You should not leave these in when firing terra cotta; they can be removed and replaced with glue after firing. If you plan to fire your terra cotta mask, do not leave any air bubbles that will explode in the kiln. Allow the finished form to dry thoroughly, then paint, polish, or stain to create your desired effect.

Make a mask with cardboard boxes cut and shaped into alligator noses, teeth, and horns painted and held together with movable brad fasteners.

You may have guessed by now that there is no end to the number of different masks you can create, and no one correct method of creating them. So get busy and make your mask!

papier-mache

cut when dry

add stiff cardboard headdress, nose, and eyelids. Adhere with papier-mache. Cut out eyes, mouth. Punch holes for Raffia or yarn.

clay beads

Home Sweet Village

Countries in western Africa, especially in coastal regions, have large bustling cities with sky-scrapers, television stations, buses, automobiles, and the same modern conveniences found in all cities. But there are still many small villages inland where people live as they have for centuries, all but untouched by the outside world. Grain is still ground to flour with large grinding stones and water is pulled from village wells. Homes are round with thatched conical tops as they have always been, and customary celebrations and rituals are still observed and enjoyed.

Activities and Projects

Create a traditional west African village in miniature. Begin with a shallow box and sprinkle the bottom with fine dirt (red or tan, if possible). Use cylindrical cardboard containers such as oatmeal boxes painted white for houses and, using the pattern given, cut cones from stiff paper for the roofs. Glue on straw for thatch. Collect some knarled sticks to make a baobob tree. Bundle them together and secure them by wrapping lightweight wire around them. Poke the end of the wire through the bottom of the box to hold the tree in place. Use salt clay to form villagers and wrap bits of colorful cloth around them for clothing. Paint on details. Add tiny versions of the ornaments, adinkra prints, and masks that are presented on previous pages. Add a mask-maker, working away from the rest of the village with his adze. Make chickens and other village animals in the same manner. Construct a well (put a tiny mirror or foil in the bottom). Put in some vegetables growing in a garden plot and children gathered 'round a storyteller. The more details you add, the better your village will be.

roof

cut

Now This Story

"Now this story—I didn't make it up" is how the Sefwi storytellers in Ghana may begin. "Who did then?" shouts the eager group. People in western Africa are great storytellers. For centuries they have used this oral tradition as a teaching tool to relate their myths about creation, their legends of ancestors, how rituals and taboos came about, and to spin yarns of humorous tricksters with moral lessons at the end. It is estimated that the Yoruba people alone have over 5,000 stories in their vast repertoire. Many people, beginning with early missionaries, have studied and recorded them. The famous Uncle Remus stories have their roots in western Africa. A good storyteller will probably include women singing and acting during a tale and will change his or her voice for different characters. The audience usually participates. Once the story is finished and the moral lesson is known, the storyteller ends, "This is my story which I have now told you. Whether it is sweet, or whether it is not sweet, take a bit of it and keep it under your pillow."